CAMPAIGN 299

ZAMA 202 BC

Scipio crushes Hannibal in North Africa

MIR BAHMANYAR

ILLUSTRATED BY PETER DENNIS
Series editor Marcus Cowper

First published in Great Britain in 2016 by Osprey Publishing,
PO Box 883, Oxford, OX1 9PL, UK
1385 Broadway, 5th Floor, New York, NY 10018, USA

E-mail: info@ospreypublishing.com
Osprey Publishing, part of Bloomsbury Publishing Plc
© 2016 Osprey Publishing Ltd

A CIP catalogue record for this book is available from the British Library.

ISBN: 978 1 4728 1421 0
PDF e-book ISBN: 978 1 4728 1422 7
e-Pub ISBN: 978 1 4728 1423 4

Editorial by Ilios Publishing Ltd, Oxford, UK (www.iliospublishing.com)
Index by Alison Worthington
Typeset in Myriad Pro and Sabon
Maps by Bounford.com
3D bird's-eye views by The Black Spot
Battlescene illustrations by Peter Dennis
Originated by PDQ Media, Bungay, UK
Printed in China through Worldprint Ltd.

16 17 18 19 20   10 9 8 7 6 5 4 3 2 1

ARTIST'S NOTE

Readers may care to note that the original paintings from which the colour
plates in this book were prepared are available for private sale. The
Publishers retain all reproduction copyright whatsoever. All enquiries
should be addressed to:
Peter Dennis, Fieldhead, The Park, Mansfield, Notts, NG18 2AT, UK
Email: magie.h@ntlworld.com
The Publishers regret that they can enter into no correspondence upon this
matter.

THE WOODLAND TRUST

Osprey Publishing are supporting the Woodland Trust, the UK's leading
woodland conservation charity, by funding the dedication of trees.

PHOTOGRAPHIC IMAGES

The photographs that appear in this work comprise images from the
author's collection and those in the public domain, unless otherwise
indicated.

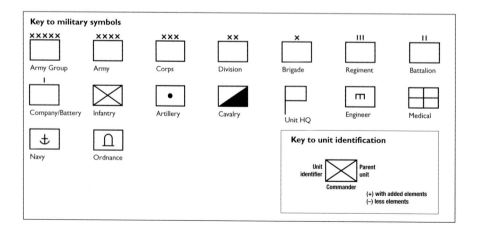

CONTENTS

ORIGINS OF THE CAMPAIGN

Three long and epic wars were waged for dominance of the Western Mediterranean between the merchant metropolis of Semitic Phoenician Carthage and the expansionist city of Rome. Both of these powers were founded by refugees – Carthage by Queen Elissa (known as Dido to the Romans) and Rome by Aeneas (who fled from Troy) – and, according to ancient legend, the two became lovers before separating.

Punic Carthage was founded on the shores of North Africa around 814 BC. Its citadel or stronghold, called Byrsa in Phoenician, was situated on a hill overlooking the Gulf of Tunis and the surrounding plains – an ideal location, with natural harbours just below the hill. Carthage may have been named after the ancient Cypriot city of Kition, founded in the 13th century BC, which was known as Qart-ḥadašt, or New City in Phoenician, to the ancients and to the Phoenician settlers who had colonised parts of the island in the 9th century BC (Soren et al. 1990, pp. 24–25).

The ruins of Ancient Carthage on the Byrsa hill.

The two lovers Aeneas and Elissa (Dido) in Carthage, imaginatively depicted by Pierre-Narcisse Guérin (1774–1833). Aeneas is recounting stories of Troy and its destruction. Guérin's original hangs in the Louvre, Paris.

The legend of the founding of Carthage, according to the Roman poet Virgil (70–19 BC) in *The Aeneid*, states that Queen Elissa had fled from the Phoenician city of Tyre in Lebanon and landed in North Africa. Here a local Berber king promised her a plot of land not to exceed the size of an oxhide (Berbers were known as Libyans to the Greeks and Romans). Cunningly, Elissa proceeded to cut the hide into strips, which she then laid out around a parcel of land on a hilltop. This became known as the Byrsa (a similar sounding Greek word meant 'oxhide').

The death of Dido, Queen of Carthage, beautifully illustrated by Giambattista Tiepolo (1696–1770). The original is in the Pushkin State Museum of Fine Arts, Moscow.

5

Virgil tells us that Queen Elissa fell in love with Aeneas, a Trojan War refugee, who, after the destruction of his city, found temporary respite in her arms. But Aeneas abandoned her in his quest for a new home, a city later founded by his descendants and called Rome. Elissa, shattered by his departure, stabbed herself with his sword just prior to immolation. As she prepared for death, Virgil continues, Elissa uttered curses against the descendants of Aeneas, which would eventually lead Carthage to war with Rome.

The legend may well have its roots in a story written by the ancient Siculo-Greek historian Timaeus (345–c.250 BC), but one in which the queen was to be forced into an undesired marriage by the local Berber king. Rather than submit to him, she threw herself into a funeral pyre which had originally been intended for an offering to the gods (Soren et al. 1990, pp. 18–19).

The wars between Carthage and Rome, instigated by the latter in 264 BC, stretched over some 120 years (44 of which were spent in campaigning) and ended with the destruction of Carthage in 146 BC. We may not be surprised to discover that prior to their great wars, Rome and Carthage had traded and had established diplomatic relations. The First Punic War (264–241 BC) was fought for hegemony over the island of Sicily but in effect signalled the beginning of a widespread war initiated by Rome in its quest for dominance of the known world. The Second Punic War (218–201 BC), sometimes called the Hannibalic War after the famous Carthaginian general Hannibal (247–c.183 BC), saw Carthage attempt to bring Rome to its knees by invading Italy and taking the war directly to the Romans. The Third Punic War (149–146 BC) witnessed the annihilation of Carthage. Each of these three conflicts was instigated and won by Rome, but Carthage was able to recover its mercantile power after the first two. The third war ended after a three-year-long siege witnessing savage street-to-street fighting before the city of Carthage was finally destroyed and its population sold into slavery.

Much of the history of Carthage will remain shrouded in mystery, for almost everything we know about this ancient city comes from its enemy, the Romans. Carthage's libraries and any narratives were given away to Numidian kings or lost during the looting once the great city finally fell.

Queen Elissa (or Dido) of Carthage's suicide, in a romantic painting by Joseph Stallaert (1825–1903) held in the Royal Museums of Fine Arts of Belgium. With her dying breath, Elissa put a curse upon Rome and paved the way towards long-standing war with the city. Aeneas's sword, with which she has stabbed herself, lies under her left arm.

Rome at the time of the Punic Wars was surrounded by 11km of walls and held an urban population totalling 90,000. Roman male citizens, aged 17 and older, numbered 292,234 in a 265 BC census while the Latins and other allies provided an additional 550,000 men for Rome's military. Approximately 3 million people, along with slaves, inhabited the peninsula under Roman control.

According to Greek historian Strabo (64/63 BC–c.AD 24) who was born in modern-day Turkey, Carthage had 700,000 residents, though estimates as low as 100,000–200,000, based on archaeological evidence, seem more likely. The entire population under its control in North Africa may have numbered 2 million (Hoyos 2015, pp. 12–15). A triple wall divided the city from the interior hinterland and massive fortifications ran along the sea. The triple walls were said to be able to house elephants and horses along with its garrison. Livy (64/59 BC–AD 17), the Roman author of a history of Rome, tells us that the walls were about 34km in length with towers every 52m. The Greco-Roman historian Appian (AD 95–165) provides a description of the fortifications during the Third Punic War:

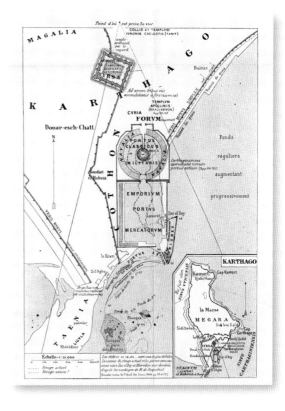

> The height of each wall was 15 meters without counting parapets and towers, which were separated from each other by a space of 60 meters, and each was divided into four stories. The depth was 10 meters. Each wall was divided vertically by two vaults, one above the other. In the lower space there were stables for 300 elephants, and alongside were receptacles for their food. Above were stables for 4,000 horses and places for their fodder and grain. There were barracks also for soldiers, 20,000 foot and 4,000 horse. (Appian 19.95)

An 1899 recreation of the ancient harbours of Carthage by French archaeologist Paul Aucler (1865–1915).

A beguiling view of Carthage, complete with lush vegetation, is presented in this 1825 work by English landscape painter David Cox (1783–1859). Cox's original is held at Birmingham Museums and Art Gallery, UK.

The natural harbours had been extended, resulting in sophisticated commercial and military facilities. The climate in North Africa thousands of years ago allowed for exceptional agriculture and Carthage became well known for it. This coupled with its world-renowned mercantile trade made Carthage a wealthy city – one which could afford formidable defences, a large fleet and expensive mercenaries.

Like Rome, Carthage conquered neighbouring territories and expanded its hegemony. Unlike Rome however, those conquered natives did not always enjoy the rights of citizenship or special privileges which Rome extended to its new subjects. One thing we do know is that Carthaginian aristocrats did intermarry with members of the Numidian royalty.

THE FIRST PUNIC WAR

The First Punic War (264–241 BC) was fought for supremacy over the island of Sicily. The war ended with Carthage ceding its claims and with Rome establishing its first, though largely autonomous, territory outside of the Italian mainland.

Before the war, Carthage was considered the most dominant naval power in the Mediterranean. Its merchants traded and established posts and colonies as far flung as Spain, Sardinia, Corsica and Sicily to name but a few. Domestically, Carthage rose to dominance by sword and trade in North Africa over the various native Berber tribes such as the Numidians, Libyans, Mauri and Gaetuli. Not much is known of the various tribes and locations as they were nomadic or semi-nomadic peoples, and it is only with the advent of the Punic Wars that some tribes are uniformly given names, even if those names were used rather loosely to describe distant tribes. During the Second Punic War the Massylii, the Masaesylii and the Mauri came to the fore. Their territories in total extended from Tripolitania to the Atlantic but were extended or reduced according to the wars they waged against each other, the Carthaginians and Romans (Ilevbare 1981, pp. 8–9).

In the meantime, Rome was busy increasing its wealth and power by subjugating neighbouring rivals. Long and hard-won wars were fought with the Samnites, Etruscans and several Greek city-states in the south of Italy. Gauls were a constant thorn in Rome's side, which would eventually lead to genocidal wars against them until they too were utterly crushed. In general, the defeated rivals were quickly absorbed into the Roman republic and would provide significant manpower and resources during the Punic Wars.

In Sicily, Carthage had previously waged campaigns against the Siculo-Greeks, and had settled somewhat comfortably for the western part of the island. During one of the many Greco-Carthaginian wars, North Africa was invaded in 310 BC by Agathocles (317–289 BC), tyrant of Syracuse and King

Samnite soldiers in a tomb fresco from Nola, 4th century BC, held in the Museo Archeologico Nazionale, Naples, Italy (inv. nr. 9363). An Oscan-speaking people, the Samnites initially allied themselves with Rome against the Gauls in 354 BC, but later became their enemies – to their eventual cost. They fought alongside Pyrrhus and Hannibal in the Pyrrhic (280–275 BC) and Second Punic wars respectively. The Samnites were wiped out in 82 BC by the Roman dictator Sulla.

of Sicily. He was defeated and retreated to Sicily, but Carthage was unable to make gains in the eastern part of the island. This would not be the only time the territories around Carthage would be invaded and the city itself besieged.

Events came to a head between the superpowers of Carthage and Rome in 288 BC when Messana (modern Messina), the Sicilian city geographically closest to the mainland of Italy, was captured by a band of Campanian mercenaries from Italy who had previously served under Agathocles. These mercenaries called themselves Mamertines after the Campanian war god Mamers, the Roman god of war Mars. They clashed with Hiero II of Syracuse (308–215 BC) who finally defeated them in 265/264 BC, forcing them back into their city (Hoyos 2015, p. 30). The Mamertines had previously allied themselves with Carthage to defeat Syracuse's ally Pyrrhus of Epirus (319/318–272 BC) in Sicily, but afterwards the Mamertines raided Carthaginian colonies on the western part of the island. Holed up in Messana and besieged by Hiero II, the mercenaries appealed for aid first to Carthage and then to Rome.

Concerns over the possibility of Carthage's hegemony spreading throughout Sicily led Rome to intervene, but in fact Rome was the power expanding its territories. By the time the Mamertines sought assistance, Rome's southerly expansion had extended, by 270 BC, to directly across the strait from the city of Messana (Hoyos 2015, p. 33). The latter was now within sight, and focused the attention of Rome. Although the First Punic War began at the behest of mercenaries, in reality it was a war fuelled by Rome's desire for military conquest.

Within a year Hiero II had been defeated by Rome, but in exchange for an alliance was acknowledged as king of Sicily. Carthage had enjoyed a presence in Sicily for 300 years and the Greeks had not been able to dislodge them

This 1791 painting by Andries Cornelis Lens (1739–1822) held in the Hermitage Museum, St Petersburg is entitled *Regulus Returning to Carthage*. Regulus was the Roman commander who was defeated and captured at the battle of Tunis in 255 BC by the Spartan mercenary captain Xanthippus. Regulus was sent to Rome on his word to return to Carthage should the Romans refuse the proposed peace treaty – a treaty he told Rome not to accept. True to his word, Regulus returned to Carthage, where he was put to death.

from the western side of the island, but Rome and Syracuse looked to change that. The war raged back and forth on land and sea, and spread to North Africa, where the invading consular Roman army and its commander, Regulus (307–250 BC), were initially successful. However, Regulus offered such harsh terms for peace that Carthage rejected them, and instead recruited the Spartan mercenary captain Xanthippus. The latter, steeped in the military tactics and prowess of Sparta, commanded a hastily raised army and in 255 BC annihilated Regulus along with his consular army at the battle of Tunis with tactics bearing similarity to the astounding double-envelopment victory Hannibal achieved during the Second Punic War at the battle of Cannae in 216 BC.

The fortunes of war ebbed and flowed, but in the end Carthage's supposed naval superiority lay shattered at the bottom of the sea and Rome, allied with Hiero II, had conquered most of Sicily. The First Punic War lasted 24 years and both powers were left exhausted. Carthage abandoned Sicily and a slew of smaller islands, returned prisoners and paid a sizeable reparation. Corsica and Sardinia, however, remained under Carthage's sphere of influence.

The self-funding war envisioned by Rome at the beginning of the conflict did not come to fruition. Rome had been forced to borrow significant funds from private citizens to gain naval superiority. For Rome, the result was painful financially as well as in terms of manpower. It may have risen to naval superiority during the war, and gained its first territory outside the mainland, but in the end it could not field another expensive fleet. It had, however, emerged victorious, and could now focus its war efforts on other, smaller, rivals. The Carthaginians, for their part, were left in such dire financial straits that they were unable to pay their mercenaries, leaving them (worryingly) stranded in North Africa. One aspect which would haunt Carthage in later conflicts was Rome's ability to exploit the resentment of the Berbers in Libya. Clearly Carthage ruled its subjects harshly, imposing heavy taxation. The neglect of such alliances would lead to further defeat.

The harbour of New Carthage (modern-day Cartagena) in southern Spain viewed from the citadel. Hasdrubal the Fair founded this city in 228/227 BC. It was later captured by Scipio. (Michelle Ricci)

THE TRUCELESS (OR LIBYAN) WAR

Shortly after the conclusion of the First Punic War, Carthage was nearly overcome by a revolt of its unpaid mercenaries following their service in Sicily and in North Africa, known as the Truceless (or Libyan) War (241–238 BC). This conflict saw 20,000 mercenaries (comprising Spaniards, Gauls, Ligurians and southern Italians as well as native conscripts) wreak havoc in North Africa; in turn, some 70,000 Libyans and Numidians, unhappy under the yoke of Carthage, were induced to join them. The rebels blockaded Carthage while laying siege to the allied cities of Utica and Hippo Acra, which eventually joined the rebellion. Finally even Carthage itself was besieged. The Carthaginians armed their citizens with all available weapons and armour, and organised and drilled them; they also repaired their fleet, and, ironically, hired more mercenaries (Riddehough 1939, p. 62).

Torture and mutilation were practised by both sides. Carthaginian armies were defeated and Hamilcar Barca (*c*.275–228 BC), the disgraced veteran commander of the latter part of the Sicilian campaign, was recalled to command. A large number of rebellious mercenaries were eventually driven into a canyon, where many starved and resorted to cannibalism before surrendering to their previous paymasters. The remaining 40,000 Libyan rebels were annihilated afterwards. The victorious Carthaginians then spent considerable energy reestablishing their authority over the rebellious territories, thus ending the war. Polybius describes the extreme nature of the war:

> This Libyan war, that had brought Carthage into such peril, resulted not only in the Carthaginians regaining possession of Libya, but in their being able to inflict exemplary punishment on the authors of the rebellion. The last scene in it was a triumphal procession of the young men leading Mathos [the Libyan rebel leader] through the town and inflicting on him all kinds of torture. This war had lasted for three years and four months, and it far excelled all wars we know of in cruelty and defiance of principle. (Polybius 1.84.5–7)

Rome took advantage of Carthage's desperation and seized Sardinia and Corsica. The North Africans were in no state to resume hostilities with Rome and had to endure further insult by agreeing to Roman demands of additional reparations to keep the peace.

THE SECOND PUNIC WAR

Having lost Sicily, Sardinia and Corsica, Carthage turned its attention elsewhere to recover from the war by developing trade and restoring domestic control in North Africa. Carthage soon expanded its territories in the Iberian Peninsula under the leadership of Hamilcar Barca, the father of Hannibal (the eldest), Hasdrubal (245–207 BC) and Mago (243–203 BC). None of these brothers would die a natural death.

The silver mines of Spain filled the Carthaginian war chests. Spanish mercenaries were heavily recruited and used in conjunction with Carthaginian troops to further increase Hamilcar's grip over the peninsula. Hamilcar died during a river crossing and his son-in-law Hasdrubal the Fair (*c*.270–221 BC) arrived from Carthage to assume leadership, as 10-year-old Hannibal was too young. Hasdrubal further consolidated Carthage's grip on the Iberian Peninsula and founded New Carthage (Cartagena) in Spain. New Carthage possessed a natural harbour and was in close proximity to local silver mines.

By 221 BC a 26-year-old Hannibal was elected by the Carthaginian army of Spain to replace Hasdrubal the Fair, who had been assassinated by a Spaniard. Hannibal consolidated his position on the Iberian Peninsula over the next few years.

Hasdrubal the Fair in a modern portrait bust in Cartagena, Spain. (Michelle Ricci)

Rome cast a weary eye on the rebirth of their enemy Carthage. Using Spanish silver and mercenary manpower, the Carthaginians reignited their trading hegemony across the Mediterranean. Rome too began to strengthen alliances: a previous agreement required Carthage not to advance north of Spain's Ebro River, but Rome signed a treaty of friendship with the town of Saguntum that lay well south of the river, a clever move which irked Carthage but avoided violating the treaty. Rome further increased hostilities with Carthage in Spain by interfering in the internal politics of Saguntum resulting in a lengthy siege of the town by Hannibal – Carthage, after all, did control most of Spain. The Spanish city never received any help from its Roman ally during the eight-month siege, which is often identified as the starting point of the Second Punic War.

Traditionally the Phoenicians were seen as the dominant naval power while Rome enjoyed land superiority, but Rome's naval arm was in fact superior to that of the Carthaginians not only during the first war but in perpetuity. The battles between the two powers were fought not on Roman territory but on Sicilian and North African soil save for a few Carthaginian naval raids on Italy. Hannibal's strategy was to take the war to Rome, to devastate its land and to destroy as many Roman armies as possible while treating Rome's allies with a gentler hand, hoping that they in turn would join his army, thereby isolating Rome further and forcing the Romans to sue for peace. To this end Hannibal marched his army from Spain to Italy overland, across rivers and over mountain ranges, including the Pyrenees and the Alps. He lost tens of thousands of men to desertion, ambushes and the elements as well as most of his elephants, but Hannibal never lost sight of the objective of ending Roman dominance, and perhaps that of seeking revenge for the seizure of Corsica and Sardinia by Rome during the Truceless War.

To safeguard Spain with its valuable silver mines and mercenary manpower, which he undoubtedly would need during the campaign, Hannibal left his brother Hasdrubal in charge with a substantial, polyglot force comprising:

Hannibal, with his father Hamilcar by his side, swears an oath of eternal animosity to the Romans as a 9-year-old child prior to his departure for Spain. The painting by Johann Heinrich Schönfeld is dated 1660 and is held at the Germanisches Nationalmuseum Nürnberg, Germany.

Carthaginian campaigns in the Mediterranean, 218–203 BC.

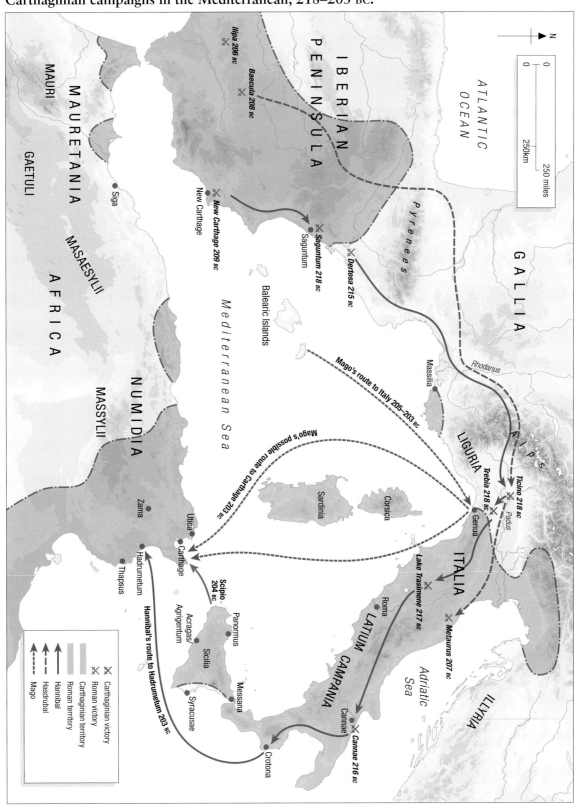

fifty quinqueremes [five banks of oars], two quadriremes [four banks] and all the triremes [three banks] … fully manned. He also gave him as cavalry Liby-Phoenicians and Libyans to the number of 450, 300 Ilergetes [Spaniards] and 1,800 Numidians drawn from the Massylii, Masaesylii, Maccoei and Maurusi [Mauri], who dwell by the ocean, and as infantry 11,850 Libyans, 300 Ligurians, and 500 Balearians, as well as 21 elephants. (Polybius 3.33.15–16)

Hannibal gazes down at the head of his brother Hasdrubal, a detail from a cycle of paintings commissioned for the Palazzo Dolfin Manin, Venice, Italy. The artist is Giovanni Battista Tiepolo (1696–1770) and the original now resides in the Kunsthistorisches Museum, Vienna, Austria.

The Romans suffered greatly during the next 15 years of Hannibal's campaign in the Italian heartland. Hannibal remained undefeated in every major engagement. His victories at Trebia (218 BC), Trasimene (217 BC) and Cannae (216 BC) humiliated the Roman generals, soldiers, citizens and their allies. The casualties the Romans suffered at Cannae alone were a staggering 45,000 infantry and 2,700 cavalry killed and 19,300 taken as prisoners of war; only 14,550 escaped the slaughter. Several commanders, both quaestors, 29 out of 48 tribunes and no fewer than 80 senators or senatorial hopefuls perished (Lazenby 1998, p. 84).

Although former Roman allies now joined the great Carthaginian general, Rome had no desire to surrender. More and more Roman and allied armies were raised to fight on various fronts – Spain, Sicily, Greece, North Africa and, of course, in Italy – and the drain on manpower was enormous. Rome's single-minded pursuit of victory, however, would remain the critical factor.

Hannibal's brothers suffered severe reverses in Spain against Publius Cornelius Scipio (236–183 BC). Hasdrubal Barca was defeated in 215 BC at Dertosa (Spain). By 206 BC, in the wake of Scipio's brilliant victory at Ilipa that year, Rome had wrested control of the Iberian Peninsula from the Barcids, thereby denying Hannibal and his brothers precious troops and funding for the continuation of the war effort. Despite being a master tactician and strategic visionary, Hannibal was unable to match either the resources, or the desire for total war, that Rome possessed. Rome was built upon its armies and its willingness to sacrifice its young while Carthage's identity was rooted in trade. In a moment of great crisis post-Cannae, according to Livy, the Romans even resorted to human sacrifices. Besieging Rome was not an option for Hannibal; Saguntum had taken eight months to reduce, without the fear of another army seeking to relieve the city.

By 205 BC Rome had contained the invasions of Italian mainlaind that Hannibal and his brother Hasdrubal had executed, recapturing key cities. Hannibal's men were worn out, and his allies were becoming fewer. To make matters worse, Hasdrubal was defeated and killed in the battle of the Metaurus (Italy) in 207 BC while attempting to reinforce

Hannibal. Hasdrubal's severed head was delivered to Hannibal; the message was clear. Hannibal, by contrast, had extended burial rites to the slain Roman generals Tiberius Sempronius Gracchus and Lucius Aemilius Paulus after Cannae.

Carthaginian forces in Sicily had been driven out by Scipio, reversing the gains achieved in the wake of Cannae. Scipio now had a naval base for launching an assault on Carthage itself, and in 204 BC he sought, and achieved, permission to do so. The move would force Hannibal's recall from Italy, setting the stage for a showdown in his homeland.

CHRONOLOGY

264–241 BC	The First Punic War.
255 BC	Xanthippus defeats Regulus at the battle of Tunis.
247 BC	Hannibal is born as Hamilcar Barca is appointed commander of the Sicilian campaign.
241–238 BC	The Truceless (or Libyan) War.
238 BC	Rome annexes Sardinia and Corsica illegally.
221 BC	Hannibal is elected commander of forces in the Iberian Peninsula.
219 BC	Saguntum is besieged by Hannibal, and captured the following year.
218–201 BC	The Second Punic War.
218 BC	The battle of Trebia, a Carthaginian victory.

217 BC	The battle of Lake Trasimene, a Carthaginian victory.
216 BC	The battle of Cannae, a Carthaginian victory.
209 BC	Scipio captures New Carthage, Spain.
208 BC	The battle of Baecula, a Roman victory.
207 BC	Hasdrubal crosses the Alps; he is killed at the battle of the Metaurus.
206 BC	The battle of Ilipa, Spain. Scipio's victory drives the Carthaginians from Spain.
205 BC	Mago Barca invades Liguria in northern Italy.
204 BC	Scipio invades North Africa from Sicily.
204 BC	The Numidian leader Masinissa joins Scipio.
203 BC	The burning of the Carthaginian camp (Utica) and battle of the Great Plains – both Romano-Numidian victories.
203 BC	Syphax, the king of the Masaesylii of western Numidia, is captured by Masinissa and Gaius Laelius.
203 BC	Hannibal and Mago are recalled to Carthage.
203 BC	Mago Barca is defeated in Cisalpine Gaul, and dies of his wounds while returning to join Hannibal in North Africa.
202 BC	The battle of Zama, a Romano-Numidian victory.
201 BC	A peace treaty ends the Second Punic War; Carthage loses its empire.
196 BC	Hannibal is elected as sufete (chief magistrate) of Carthage.
195 BC	Masinissa raids Carthaginian territories.
195 BC	Hannibal leaves Carthage for exile; Rome is alarmed by Carthage's growing prosperity.
186 BC	Scipio enters self-imposed exile.
185 BC	Death of Scipio.
183/182 BC	Hannibal commits suicide at the court of Prusias in Libyssa, Bithynia (near modern Gebze in Turkey).
151 BC	Carthage declares war on Masinissa.
149–146 BC	The Third Punic War, ending in the annihilation of Carthage.

OPPOSING COMMANDERS

CARTHAGINIAN

Born in 247 BC, **Hannibal Barca** moved to Spain at the age of 10. Around this time he made a vow to his father never to be friends to the Romans, or so the ancient sources tell us. He would not return to Carthage until he turned 45. In Spain he learned the art of war, first under the command of his father and then Hasdrubal the Fair, Hamilcar's son-in-law, who had succeeded the latter after his death during a river crossing. Well educated and multilingual, Hannibal enjoyed an excellent reputation with the men – Carthaginians, Liby-Phoenicians, Numidians, Greeks, Balearians and Spaniards to name but the major ones. The army which had conquered most of Spain was a polyglot grouping and Hannibal was comfortable commanding it. At the age of 26, following the assassination of Hasdrubal the Fair, he was elected commanding general by his army.

An interpretation of Hannibal by Franco-Belgian sculptor Sébastien Slodtz (1655–1726). The sculpture was made in 1704 and is at the Louvre in Paris, France. Hannibal is counting the rings of the fallen Roman knights at Cannae. Note the captured, inverted Roman standard in his right hand. (Marie-Lan Nguyen)

Hannibal knew Rome would always interfere in Carthaginian territories, including the Iberian Peninsula, and his strategy was to take the inevitable war to the Roman heartland. The First Punic War had been fought primarily on Sicilian and North African soil. This war would be different and Hannibal's breathtaking crossing of the Alps into Italy by 218 BC (which Hasdrubal would mirror 11 years later) stunned the world, as did his masterfully executed battle tactics during his remaining years in Italy.

One factor that sets Hannibal apart from most of his contemporaries is the fact that he was raised in a multicultural environment, and that a host of diverse mercenaries served with him. He reputedly had a sharp wit and spoke well, and was fluent in Greek and Latin. Communicating effectively was instrumental in commanding a polyglot army whose soldiers probably knew but a smattering of Phoenician commands.

Hannibal's formative years also gave him an excellent tactical education. He was competent as a naval commander and he was well trained and experienced in guerrilla warfare including reconnaissance and ambuscade to the execution of combined arms on the

A modern portrait bust of Hannibal at Cartagena, Spain. (Michelle Ricci)

fields of battle with its tactical variances. Even siege craft was familiar to him. Each type of warfare required different logistics and training, but all required intelligence gathering. The latter was instrumental in his army crossing the Alps and seeking out allies on his voyage into Italy, and certainly reconnaissance was required regularly while operating on the mainland. By the time the Second Punic War began in earnest, Hannibal was a veteran commander who could impose a unified command structure, and one who was capable of integrating new foreign fighters and their unique techniques of war into his battle lines and tactics.

Hannibal was no ordinary commander: he was extraordinary. Polybius comments on the effectiveness of his leadership: 'though he was for 17 years engaged in actual warfare, and though he had to make his way through numerous barbaric tribes, and to employ innumerable men of different nationalities in what appeared desperate and hazardous enterprises, he was never made the object of a conspiracy by any of them, nor deserted by any of those who had joined him and put themselves under his command' (Polybius 23.13). Although desertion was commonplace, Hannibal's ability to maintain an army in hostile terrain remains striking. No doubt a core of veterans stayed with Hannibal out of loyalty. Others may have been inspired by his well-attested bravery, temperance and restraint. His armies were habitually inferior in numbers but superior in fighting spirit, and Hannibal maintained

The defining image of Hannibal remains his crossing of the Alps with elephants. This depiction from the mid-1620s, currently in a private collection, has been attributed to the leading painter of the classical French baroque style, Nicolas Poussin (1594–1665).

A powerful, but fantastical, image of Hannibal at Cannae, showing the collection of rings from the slain knights after the battle. Intaglio by Heinrich Leutemann (1824–1905) from the 1877 book *Rom* by Wilhelm Wagner.

morale by leading often from the front (he was wounded during the siege of Saguntum), lightening the mood of his officers (as he did prior to engaging the vastly superior Roman legions at Cannae) and sharing the physical deprivations of his men.

We do not know for sure what Hannibal looked like – neither in terms of physical appearance nor ethnicity. No identifiable images remain of him: coins that may have shown his image were melted down to mint new Roman coins. Any native written records of him were either destroyed or handed over to the Numidian kings and are now lost. The ancient authors do not give us a physical description of Hannibal other than that he was missing an eye. The archaeologist and historian Patrick Hunt, whilst stressing how little evidence we have in this matter, notes Hannibal's Phoenecian ancestors had quite possibly 'intermixed in DNA with peoples then living in North Africa … so we shouldn't deny any possible Africanization of the region of Carthage' (Hunt 2015).

A 19th-century depiction of the battlefield of Cannae, where the Romans lost a generation of senators and citizens.

19

By the time Hannibal returned to North Africa in 203 BC, he had lost everything: his brothers, his home and base in Spain and lastly the war, for Hannibal surely understood after close to two decades of fighting Rome that he lacked the resources for ultimate victory. Defeating the invading Roman army in North Africa might be possible, and perhaps even an honourable albeit painful truce might be negotiated, but the fact that Rome should have surrendered, but did not, several years earlier must have made things clear to Hannibal. The outcome of the Second Punic War was thus a forgone conclusion. Any victory over the Roman legions in North Africa could only be a temporary respite.

The Numidian commander **Syphax**, ally of Hannibal, was the king of the Masaesylii, a tribe whose western territory in North Africa faced Spain, and were allied at various times to Carthage (Livy 24.48.2). Although Syphax did not participate at Zama, he was instrumental in the events leading up to it.

Syphax had been courted by Scipio's father around 213/212 BC. He eventually accepted Roman military advisors, led by the centurion Lucius Statorius, to train his forces engaged in a war against the eastern-based Massylii, who were ruled at that time by King Gaia and his ally Carthage. When King Gaia died, his sons, including Masinissa and Navaras, began fighting over the inheritance of the kingdom (Hoyos, p. 169). After the successful Roman campaign in Spain, Scipio sailed from New Carthage to Syphax's capital city of Siga on the Numidian coast. Here too was the Carthaginian general Hasdrubal, son of Gisco, courting the alliance of Syphax, who by now was winning the war for Numidia against Masinissa.

Syphax, as well as his enemy Masinissa, were approached yet again by Gaius Laelius at Scipio's behest around 206 BC in preparation for the Roman invasion of North Africa. While Masinissa joined the Romans after having met the advance raiding party under Laelius (who landed in North Africa in 205 BC), Syphax, now victorious over Masinissa, married Sophoniba, the daughter of Hasdrubal, son of Gisco, thereby cementing his relationship with Carthage. Sophoniba was the third Carthaginian aristocrat to marry into Numidian royalty (Hoyos, pp. 201–02).

Syphax and his army were defeated twice: firstly when his camp was attacked and burnt to the ground in a night raid, and secondly at the battle of the Great Plains in 203 BC. He fled the latter, but was eventually captured and sent to Italy where, according to Livy, he died sickened by grief in 201 BC at Tibur (Tivoli, Italy).

ROMAN

Publius Cornelius Scipio was born in 236 BC and died, around the same time as Hannibal, in 183 BC, on his farm in Liternum, Campania (now Patria, Italy). Much like Hannibal, Scipio was of aristocratic heritage, and he too lost family during the Second Punic War (his father Publius Scipio and his uncle Gnaeus Cornelius Scipio Calvus were killed by Hasdrubal in Spain, while his prospective father-in-law Lucius Aemilius Paulus was slain at Cannae).

We are first told of the young Scipio, in both Livy and Polybius (the latter quoting Scipio's friend Gaius Laelius), during the clash at the Ticinus River in November 218 BC against forward elements of Hannibal's army – the Numidian light cavalry. His father was wounded and in danger of being flanked when young Scipio dashed to his rescue and affected an escape.

Scipio survived the carnage at Cannae and shortly after the death of his father was given command over the legions destined to invade Spain in 210 BC. The task at hand against Hasdrubal was to defeat the Carthaginians, thereby preventing further revenues and manpower from reaching Hannibal. In Scipio's mind his mission was not defensive in nature but to take the fight to the seemingly invincible enemy. He accomplished this by training his army well, no doubt utilising his experiences of having fought Hannibal in Italy. Envelopments as well as ruses and tactical changes just prior to and during the battles proved decisive. He captured the seemingly impregnable city of New Carthage, gaining stores and supplies, Spanish hostages, control of the local silver mines and a splendid harbour and now possessed a base for an advance further south. He defeated Hasdrubal convincingly at Baecula in 208 BC, and understood the imperative to alienate the Carthaginians as much as possible from the Numidians. To that effect, Scipio freed Masinissa's nephew Massiva after Baecula and sent him back with gifts of honour (Hoyos 2015, p. 179). Of course Scipio was clever enough to also reach out to Syphax, king of the Masaesylii in Numidia.

A profile of Scipio Africanus, held in the Bode-Museum, Berlin, Germany. (Daderot)

Scipio also quelled a mutiny among his troops before crossing into Sicily in 205 BC to train a new army along with some survivors of Cannae, who had been banished to the island in disgrace. In Sicily he planned his attack against Carthage itself. Much like Hannibal, Scipio decided to take the war to the enemy's homeland, showing him to be an innovative, daring and courageous battlefield commander of the highest order.

The painting entitled *Scipio Africanus Freeing Massiva* (Masinissa's nephew) by Giovanni Battista Tiepolo beautifully captures the value Scipio placed on securing Numidian allies in his quest to defeat Hannibal and Carthage. Without the Numidians, Scipio would not have won the battle at Zama. According to the artistic conventions of the time, the high-ranking Numidians are depicted with 'European' features. Tiepolo's original is held at the Walters Art Museum in Baltimore, USA.

The excavated ruins of New Carthage (Cartagena, Spain). When Scipio captured the Barcid stronghold, the Romans were uncontrolled in their slaughter and rape of the inhabitants. (Michelle Ricci)

According to ancient sources, **Gaius Laelius** (*c*.235–*c*.160 BC) was Scipio's closest friend, 'who from his youth up to the end had participated in his every word and deed' (Polybius 10.3.2.). We know little of his youth and are only aware of some of his commands and conduct during the war.

We know Scipio brought Laelius along for the campaign in Spain and that Laelius was in command of 35 quinqueremes during the capture of New Carthage. Additionally we are told that he was sent to Rome to deliver the news of the capture of the city along with that of Carthaginian aristocrats (Hoyos 2015, pp. 175–76).

During the battle of Baecula, Laelius led the Roman left wing against Hasdrubal's right flank while Scipio executed the same manoeuvre on the other flank, as the velites and some line infantry pinned Hasdrubal's near impregnable front. During the campaigns he also commanded various cavalry detachments – something Laelius would repeat to great effect during the last battle of the Second Punic War.

After the successful conclusion of the Spanish campaign, Laelius raided the Libyan coast while an army was being trained in Sicily for the invasion of North Africa. There he was contacted by the now fugitive and wounded Masinissa, who had been defeated by Syphax. At Scipio's behest, Laelius cemented a bond of trust. Masinissa promised to help the Romans, despite the reduced numbers of troops he could supply. Nonetheless, an alliance existed and the Romans badly needed quality horsemen in their campaign against Carthage and Hannibal.

Throughout his career Gaius Laelius proved to be an exceptional commander and right-hand man to Scipio. He continued to carve out a political career in the years following the Second Punic War, rising to the consulship in 190 BC, a role he shared with Scipio's brother. In later life, he befriended the historian Polybius, and was able to share many details of Scipio's life with him.

Masinissa was born *c.*238 BC and died in 148 BC. He was a prince of the Massyli Numidians, who were allied to Carthage. Raised in Carthage, he subsequently fought the Romans in Italy, notably at Cannae, and in Spain. Courted by Romans and Carthaginians alike throughout the Second Punic War, he ultimately joined the Romans in a bid to reverse his fortunes and defeat his rival Syphax, the pro-Carthaginian ruler of the Masaesylii, in a war for control of Numidia. Scipio, ever aware of political nuances, released Masinissa's nephew Massiva, who had been captured after the battle of Baecula – even though Massiva had played a part in the deaths of Scipio's father and uncle (Hoyos 2015, p. 201).

A coin showing the head of Masinissa, who managed to unite the eastern and western tribes to become the first King of Numidia. Fittingly for his role at Zama, a horse is depicted on the reverse side.

Until Scipio's consular army invaded North Africa in 204 BC, Syphax held the upper hand over Masinissa. The latter had become a fugitive in North Africa, with but a few followers, when he met Gaius Laelius, who was conducting raids along the Libyan coast ahead of the invasion. Masinissa promised to support the Roman war effort as best as he could while Rome declared its support for his claim to the Numidian throne.

In the wake of the Roman landing in North Africa, Masinissa's ranks grew from a few hundred to around 10,000 cavalry and infantry. These troops proved to be crucial in the battle against Hannibal at Zama. Masinissa's experience and his desire to secure a Roman victory, and thus his throne, were both of great value to Scipio.

Masinissa had fallen in love with Syphax's wife Sophoniba, who was said to be able to seduce and control men. Masinissa married her but was forced, or persuaded, by Scipio and Laelius to send her to Rome to suffer the indignity of a Roman triumph. Instead, Masinissa provided poison, which according to legend she gladly took.

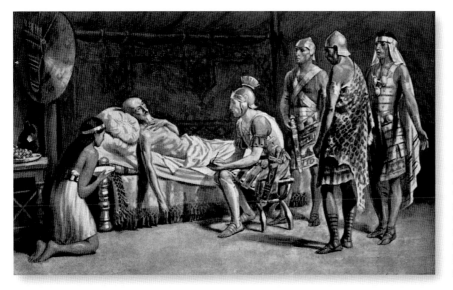

Scipio at the deathbed of Masinissa, a lithograph by A. C. Weatherstone (1888–1929). Here, King Masinissa is around 90 years of age, and is asking Scipio Aemilianus (185–129 BC) to oversee the division of his kingdom between his three sons.

OPPOSING PLANS

THE INVASION OF NORTH AFRICA

The strategic situation of the western Mediterranean by 205 BC was clear cut: Rome had contained Hannibal in the Italian peninsula, driven the Carthaginians out of Iberia and now controlled Sardinia, Corsica and, most importantly, Sicily. The original vision of the elder Scipio – to take the war to the enemy – could now be realised.

Scipio had been granted permission by the Roman senate to take volunteers and penal legions and mould them into an invasion force based in Sicily. He

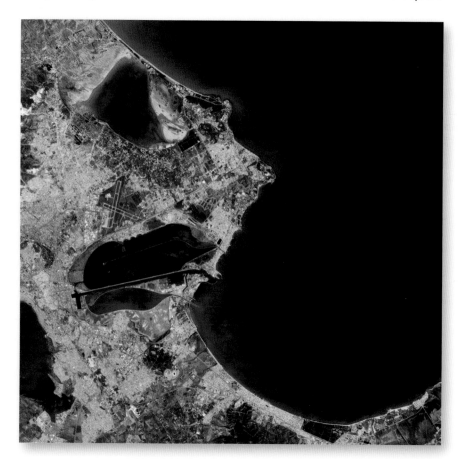

A NASA image of the area occupied by the ancient city of Carthage, what is today Tunis.

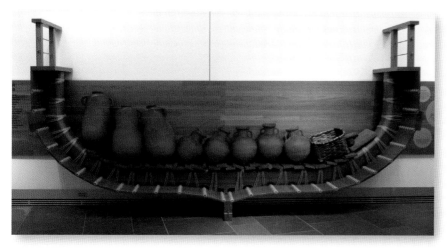

A cross-section of a Roman boat carrying amphorae, located at the Museo Nacional de Arqueología Subacuática, Cartagena, Spain. This type of vessel may very well have carried Roman forces and supplies to Scipio in North Africa. (Michelle Ricci)

took his time to recruit and train enough men, to have a logistical system in place and gather enough intelligence while firming up his alliance with Masinissa. Perhaps he knew that invading North Africa would force Hannibal to abandon Italy and would banish the 'scourge of Rome' once and for all.

The exploratory raids west of Carthage conducted by Gaius Laelius in 205 BC, while Scipio was still preparing for a full-scale invasion, served to gather intelligence, and helped strengthen the alliance with the Numidian Prince Masinissa (aided by the fact that Syphax had spurned Rome and decided to marry into Carthaginian royalty). Scipio was fully aware that any success in North Africa required Numidian support, and with this the Romano-Numidian army could very well engineer a situation in which the rebellious Libyans might join them.

Carthage's political leadership was shocked by the appearance of Roman troops on their continent. Although previous wars with the Sicilians and Romans had seen multiple invasions, they perhaps rightly had assumed that Hannibal's presence in mainland Italy should have prevented such a daring assault. Preparations were hastily made for the oncoming conflict. A request was made to King Philip of Macedon to invade Sicily, but this did not materialise. In addition, Carthaginian troops were sent to Italy to attempt to reignite war on the Italian mainland, but this had little effect.

At the end of a long year of preparation, Scipio's well-trained and (for the most part) experienced main invasion force boarded their transport ships for the crossing from Sicily to North Africa. They landed near Utica in 204 BC. At its core were the survivors of the battle of Cannae, who were eager and confident to put their shame behind them and to defeat Rome's greatest enemy. Scipio's forces were soon harassed by Numidians under Syphax, who remained loyal to Carthage. Scipio also sent 'message after message to Masinissa explaining how the Carthaginians had violated the treaty, and urging him to mobilise as strong a force as possible and make haste to join him' (Polybius 15.4.4–5).

A replicated cross-section of an ancient supply ship, showing how such vessels were loaded, in the Museo Nacional de Arqueología Subacuática, Cartagena, Spain. (Michelle Ricci)

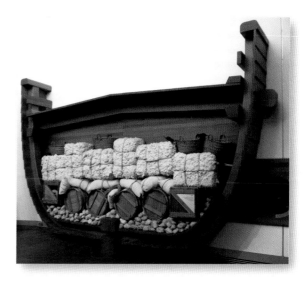

THE BURNING OF THE CAMP, AND THE GREAT PLAINS, 203 BC

In 203 BC the Romans along with the Numidians of Masinissa destroyed two Carthaginian and Numidian armies – one with a night attack on the Carthaginian camp at Utica, supposedly during a truce, and the other at the battle of the Great Plains.

The Carthaginians were led by Hasdrubal, son of Gisco, who harassed Scipio's forces using cavalry raids in 204 BC until Scipio quashed these troops at Salaeca. In the autumn of that year Scipio laid siege to the city of Utica. This in turn forced Hasdrubal and Syphax to show their two large armies, leading Scipio to retreat from the city and prepare for winter quarters. Hasdrubal and Syphax also set up their winter camps, which were mostly made of wood, and in the lull that ensued Syphax attempted to negotiate a truce with the Romans. The year turned, and as spring approached, Scipio launched a surprise attack on the Carthaginian and Numidian camps, burning them to the ground. The Carthaginians and Numidians were caught unawares, and many were slaughtered or burnt to death: the Romans had blocked the exits.

As Hasdrubal and Syphax withdrew to lick their wounds and begin replacing their losses, some 4,000 Celtiberian mercenaries arrived from the Iberian Peninsula to bolster the Carthaginian and allied ranks. Soon, the Carthaginian–Numidian army had been revived to battle strength. Scipio, for his part, continued his aggressive tactics and marched from Utica westwards, to seek out and defeat the enemy.

The two sides met at the battle of the Great Plains. The Roman cavalry charge routed the Carthaginian and Spanish infantry in Hasdrubal's centre.

Syphax was hunted down and captured by forces under Masinissa and Laelius during the fall of the city of Cirta. Syphax's loss had dealt a crippling blow to the Carthaginian cavalry capability. Scipio then wisely proclaimed Masinissa the King of Numidia, rewarding him for his loyalty. Syphax, in contrast, was shipped off to Rome for triumphal humiliation, along with his son and other Carthaginian leaders.

Scipio Africanus Accepting the Surrender of King Syphax, a painting (*c.*1512) by Bernardino Fungai (1460–1516). The original is held at the Hermitage Museum, St Petersburg. (Francesco Bini)

Scipio's campaign in North Africa proved to be brutal. Towns and cities willing to surrender were not permitted to do so but were reduced to ash, and the citizenry sold into slavery – the first act in the Phoenician holocaust. Although all appeared lost to the Carthaginians, they had one last option for turning the tide in their favour: the recall of Hannibal and his army of veterans to the homeland.

THE RETURN OF HANNIBAL, 203 BC

Hannibal was recalled from Italy in 203 BC. Along with his veteran Bruttians, a number of mercenaries previously under the command of Mago Barca joined him upon his return to Carthaginian territory. Hannibal landed near Hadrumctum about 120km south of Carthage along the coast. Here he assembled his army and also secured the loyalty of a few Numidian chieftains to provide him with a proper scouting force. How much of Hannibal's army was composed of the survivors of the two previous defeats is unknown, but we can assume some of them had indeed been present at the previous engagements. Carthaginian recruiters scoured territories for mercenaries but the situation must have been dire.

Strategically the situation had been won by Rome and one can only assume Hannibal's strategy called for either a peace before the battle or a successful campaign against Scipio that would force peace. Losing this battle might very well end in disaster for Carthage. However, his army was not in good shape. He needed time, but the invaders were ravaging the countryside and the internecine war between the Numidians was a considerable problem. Polybius tell us:

> When the people of Carthage saw the cities in their territory being sacked, they sent a message to Hannibal begging him to act without delay, to come to close quarters with the enemy, and bring the matter to the decision of battle. He bade the messengers in answer 'to confine their attention to other matters, and to leave such things to him, for he would choose the time for fighting himself.' Some days afterwards he broke up his quarters at Hadrumetum, and pitched his camp near Zama, a town about five days' march to the west of Carthage. (Polybius 15.5)

Tactically it did not matter very much where the battle would be fought, for Hannibal's army was not a well-trained one, with the exception of his veterans and perhaps some of the mercenaries. The citizen levy could only do so much. The large contingent of enemy Numidians would prevent Hannibal from enjoying tactical advantages on the field of battle as had been the case at Lake Trasimene, for example. The Romans had the eyes and ear of Masinissa's cavalry while Hannibal was feeling the loss of Syphax. Polybius notes:

> Hannibal at this time was very poorly off for cavalry and sent to a certain Numidian called Tychaeus, who was a relative of Syphax, and was thought to have the best cavalry in Africa, begging him to help him and join in saving the situation, as he knew well that, if the Carthaginians won, he could retain his principality, but if the Romans were victors, he would risk losing his life too, owing to Masinissa's greed of power. Accordingly, Tychaeus was prevailed on by this appeal and came to Hannibal with a body of 2,000 horse. (Polybius 15.3)

And thus the stage was set for the climactic battle.

The museum in Cartagena, Spain has been built to mirror the height of the walls of New Carthage, which stood at 10m tall. The walls of Carthage proper were said to be even higher, at 14m. (Michelle Ricci)

The approach to Zama, 204–202 BC.

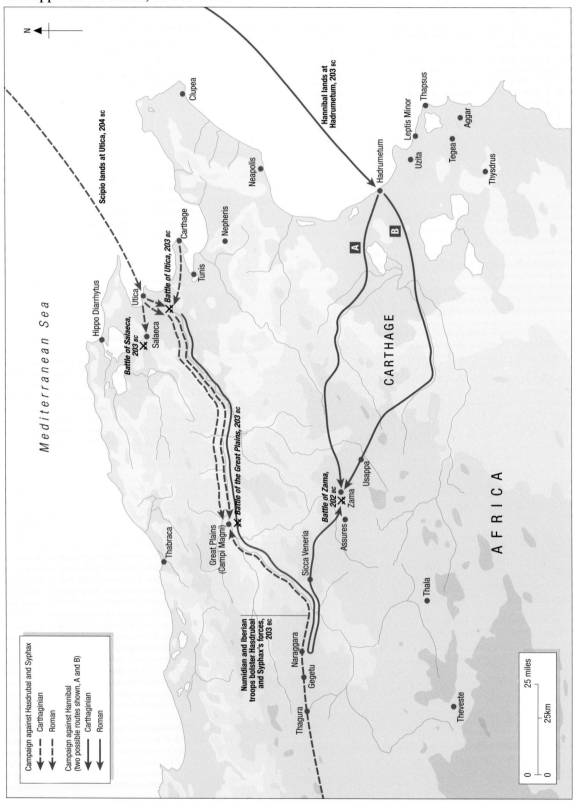

OPPOSING FORCES

THE ROMAN ARMY AT ZAMA

Scipio's consular army in North Africa in all likelihood comprised four legions including two Italian allied ones. Livy informs us that two of these were the V and VI Roman legions consisting of the vanquished and publicly shamed survivors of the battle of Cannae some 14 years earlier. This is a long time to be absent from campaigning, and we do know these two legions were stationed in Sicily and were perhaps further bloodied battling against Hiero II's successor Hieronymus, who sought to reclaim Sicilian territories for Syracuse. How many actual survivors were still enrolled in the two disgraced legions is unknown. J. F. Lazenby describes them as 'the most experienced soldiers in the Roman army, and Scipio knew that Cannae had not really been lost through any cowardice of their's – having served with them at that battle, he may well have had a fellow-feeling for them' (Lazenby 1998, p. 203). Perhaps even Scipio suffered not only from the social disgrace of having been a survivor of Cannae but its emotional impact as well, adding a further impetus or desire to redeem himself. The Cannae veterans probably made up the ranks of the principes and triarii.

The paper strength size of a Roman legion was 4,200 infantry and 200–300 cavalry. Each legion had 3,000 line infantry soldiers composed of 1,200 front rankers called hastati, 1,200 second rankers and more experienced soldiers called principes and 600 veteran, spear-carrying triarii in the third and final rank. Light infantry skirmishers called velites numbered 1,200. An allied legion provided the same number of infantry but the cavalry contingent was between 600 and 900 strong. One can see the weakness of the Roman consular army: a lack of cavalry for scouting, harassing and striking at enemy forces. In total, the paper strength of the invading force could have been 16,800 infantry and 1,600–2,400 in cavalry.

In 203 BC the Numidian Prince Masinissa may have provided, before the engagement at Zama, between 200 and 2,000 mounted soldiers to the Roman invasion force. By the time of Zama, his force had risen to between 4,000 and 6,000 cavalry accompanied by 6,000 foot. The successful turn of events against his rival Syphax certainly helped recruit more disenchanted Numidians to Masinissa's force. Thus the combined paper strength of the Romano-Numidian army totalled (at the upper end) 22,800 foot and 6,400–9,400 mounted troops, not including Prince Dacamas and his 1,600 horsemen.

The Roman legions

The ancient authors chronicling the Punic Wars state that the Roman and Italian legions fought in the same manner. A front ranker, a hastatus, would understand his function and deployment in any legion. It will suffice then to look only at a generic Roman legion to understand how they functioned on the field of battle.

The legion was divided into ten sub-units called maniples. Each maniple or manipulus was administratively subdivided in two centuriae equal in strength. The front was called the centuria prior and the rear one the centuria posterior (Fields 2007, p. 37). Each centuria comprised 60 men. In formation each manipulus had a 20-man front that was six ranks deep – a total of 120 soldiers.

The Roman infantry was the centrepiece during battle. The legions as we have seen were infantry heavy and very weak in cavalry. On the battlefield the army was almost always anchored on either side by its cavalry groups. The infantry deployment in the field comprised a three-deep battle line, a triple *acies*, with skirmishers (velites) scattered in front of it.

The velites were lightly armed troops who screened the infantry and engaged enemy light infantry during the opening stages of a battle. In addition, they acted as camp guards, conducted reconnaissance missions along with horsemen, foraged and, when required, engaged in hand-to-hand combat with enemy infantry, as witnessed in the battles in the Iberian Peninsula. The skirmishers were the youngest as well as the poorest of military eligible males – the exceptionally poor served in the navy. Polybius recounts that these boys were ordered to carry a sword, javelins and a small round shield called a parma for deflecting incoming missiles. For additional protection these boys were supposed to wear plain helmets which lacked any features such as feathers or horsehairs, but some velites decorated them with wolfskins or other fur so that their commander could identify them more easily when they demonstrated their courage in combat. Their javelins were made of wood and metal: 'The wooden shaft of the javelin measures about two cubits

A diagram of a Roman legion, detailing the various maniples and velites. The cavalry wings are correctly positioned on the flanks of the legion. Note the gap behind the triarii at the bottom of the image. (Anne S. K. Brown Military Collection, Brown University Library)

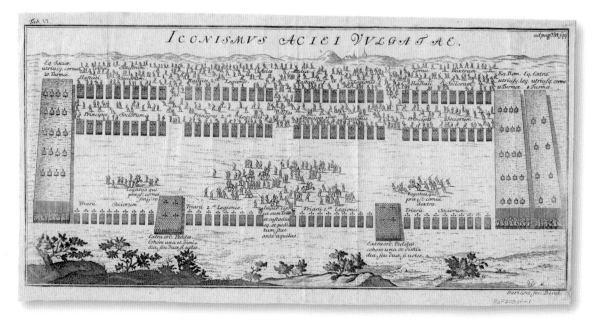

[90cm] in length and is about a finger's breadth in thickness; its head is a span [22.8cm] long hammered out to such a fine edge that it is necessarily bent by the first impact, and the enemy is unable to return it. If this were not so, the missile would be available for both sides' (Polybius 6.22.4–5). Interestingly, the velites were divided equally among the maniples, no doubt helping create a bond of brotherhood.

The first rank of line infantry in the traditional Polybian-era legion was made up of younger males, older and arguably wealthier, and perhaps more experienced, than the velites. These front-line foot soldiers were called the hastati, which translates as spearmen. The spear was a weapon used before the Punic Wars and more suitable for classical phalanx warfare made famous by the Greeks. The Roman army was ever evolving and spears were eventually replaced by two types of throwing pila: one fine and the other stout. The pilum was constructed in two parts, one of which was a long, sharp-pointed metal shaft attached to a piece of wood; this pilum would bend upon impact and would not only become useless to the enemy but, if impacted upon a wooden shield, would also drag it down with its weight, exposing the body of the enemy combatant. Polybius presents a detailed account of these fearsome weapons:

A classic Montefortino helmet. (Michelle Ricci)

> The pila are of two sorts — stout and fine. Of the stout ones some are round and a palm's length [7.5cm] in diameter and others are a palm square. Fine pila, which they carry in addition to the stout ones, are like moderate-sized hunting spears, the length of the haft in all cases being about three cubits [1.3m]. Each is fitted with a barbed iron head of the same length as the haft. This they attach so securely to the haft, carrying the attachment halfway up the latter and fixing it with numerous rivets, that in action the iron will break sooner than become detached, although its thickness at the bottom where it comes into contact with the wood is a finger's breadth and a half; such great care do they take about attaching it firmly. (Polybius 6.23.8–11)

The hastatus used a large oval shield, a scutum, to cover his body and this was one of the primary reasons for the success of the Roman army as a whole and the fighting man individually; Polybius notes that the size and strength of the scutum presented difficulties to the enemy (15.15.7–8). As a collective unit the maniples could face towards the direction of any attack and present a front; this was accomplished by individual units turning towards danger in a single movement. The shield therefore was not only an excellent piece of defensive equipment but it also bolstered the individual soldier's morale, for he knew its construction could survive most blows as well as stone and small rock projectiles. In his description of the Roman soldier, Polybius begins his narrative

Polybian legion and plebeian maniple in the Second Punic War.

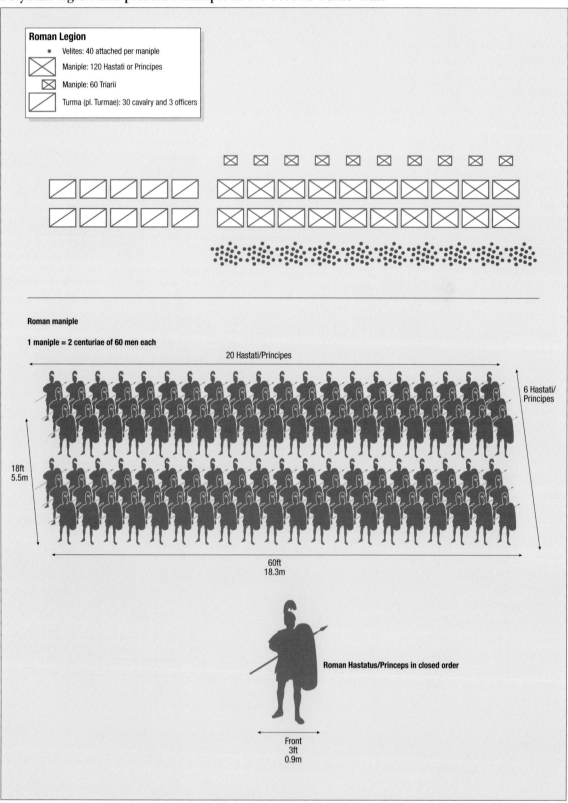

Roman Legion

- Velites: 40 attached per maniple
- Maniple: 120 Hastati or Principes
- Maniple: 60 Triarii
- Turma (pl. Turmae): 30 cavalry and 3 officers

Roman maniple

1 maniple = 2 centuriae of 60 men each

20 Hastati/Principes

6 Hastati/Principes

18ft
5.5m

60ft
18.3m

Roman Hastatus/Princeps in closed order

Front
3ft
0.9m

with the scutum, demonstrating the value he places on it. He describes it as convex, 75cm wide by 120cm long. The rim was a palm's width (6cm) having two planks glued together with its outermost surface covered in canvas and then with calfskin. Additionally, the upper and lower rims were reinforced with iron edgings whose purpose it was to protect the soldier from downward slashes of weapons wielded by the enemy. When the shield was rested on the ground, the lower rim protected it from possible damage. The centre of the scutum featured an iron boss, which protected the shield bearer's hand on the inside and also served as an offensive weapon which could be smashed into an enemy combatant.

The rest of the panoply included a Spanish-style sword called a gladius. The pila may also have originated in Spain. The gladius hung over the right thigh and it was an excellent close-quarter battle weapon for thrusting at exposed parts of the enemy fighter. Polybius says the sword's edges 'cut effectually, as the blade is very strong and firm'. He also notes that they wore brass helmets, and greaves. The former was topped by a circle of purple and black feathers about a cubit [c.44cm] high, making the soldiers seem much taller. The hastatus also wore a brass square breastplate to protect his heart known as the pectorale. It was a span (22.8cm) square in size (a span measured from thumb to little finger). This allowed the individual fighter greater mobility and flexibility, unencumbered by heavier armour.

A bronze two-part cuirass, from the British Museum, London. Such armour could well have been worn by Romans and Carthaginians. (Marie-Lan Nguyen)

The second rank of a legion comprised older, more experienced men who were identically equipped to the hastati but were called principes.

The third and last rank, the triarii, was composed of veteran soldiers equipped in the same fashion as the hastati and principes who were armed with 2.4m–2.75m-long hastae (spears) instead of pila. We are informed by Polybius that the wealthier soldiers with assets above 10,000 drachmas wore a coat of ring mail called a lorica instead of the pectoral (Polybius 6.22–23). Modern commentators have extrapolated from the ancient general and author Xenophon that half a Greek drachma per day provided a comfortable subsistence for poorer citizens, in essence for the head of a household in 355 BC. Only veteran soldiers, who had accumulated spoils in their campaigns and earned sufficiently well could afford ring mail. This last line of the Roman legion was also the smallest of the maniples: a single manipulus composed of triarii never exceeded 60 men, exactly half the size of a regular manipulus.

The infantry soldier had to serve for 16 years before he turned 46. The Roman army was forged on the anvil of near continuous war and although punishment for failure was severe, from beatings, to death by decimation or serving out the remaining years in exile from Italy, the Romans did value individual acts of bravery and therefore issued various awards for this.

The backbone of the command structure comprised the centurions, who were elected on merit and presumably were veterans. These small-unit leaders in turn selected optiones – centurions who technically were rearguard officers. Each manipulus then had two centurions and two optiones. The centurions also selected two of the best soldiers to be the standard bearers for the manipulus. Polybius states that 'the centurions not so much to be venturesome and daredevil as to be natural leaders, of a steady and sedate spirit. They do not desire them so much to be men who will initiate attacks and open the battle, but men who will hold their ground when worsted and hard-pressed and be ready to die at their posts' (6.24.8).

Cavalry

The Roman and Latin/allied cavalry was small and composed of well-to-do citizens and allies who more easily could afford the purchase and maintenance of the animals. The cavalry group of 300 was divided into ten squadrons, or turmae. The turmae also had three officers called decuriones and three rear-guard optiones.

The panoply for the wealthy cavalry, or equites, is given by Polybius once again. Before the Punic Wars the cavalry was unarmoured and thus gravely exposed in close combat as they fought almost naked. Their ox-hide shield was ineffective and did not last long on campaign, especially when it became wet, and their spear was of such inferior quality that it was very difficult to hit a target; sometimes the motion of the horse would actually break the spear. The butt-end spikes so commonly found in hoplite spears were also absent, meaning that once the spear's head shattered, it became unusable. As always the Roman military was quick to adopt other, more successful, weapons systems and in this case the cavalry copied the arms and armour of the Greek cavalry – a sturdy spear featuring a butt spike, and Greek shields capable of withstanding not only blows but also the stress of campaigning. In general terms, however, the equites were better at shock actions such as charging than scouting and harassing, as they were more heavily armed and on bigger horses than their Numidian counterparts. A cavalry soldier served for ten years.

One should note that the army was a paid army – in salary as well as plunder. Rome also used mercenaries, foreign deserters and elephants in its wars.

Part of the marble Altar of Domitius Ahenobarbus dating from the late 2nd century BC, currently on display at the Louvre, Paris. An officer stands at centre left, with Roman soldiers on the far left – note the size of their shields. The plaque depicts the Roman census.

The martial arts of the Roman infantryman

The legion lined up in a checkerboard pattern with skirmishers to the front and cavalry on its flanks. Polybius provides a description of the martial arts of the common Roman foot soldier:

> To speak of the peculiarities of the Roman equipment and system of formation … each [Roman] soldier with his arms occupies a space of three feet [0.9m] in breadth, but as in their mode of fighting each man must move separately, as he has to cover his person with his long shield, turning to meet each expected blow, and as he uses his sword both for cutting and thrusting it is obvious that a looser order is required, and each man must be at a distance of at least three feet [0.9m] from the man next to him in the same rank and those in front of and behind him, if they are to be of proper use. (Polybius 18.30.5–8)

We may deduce that there are two formations: one a closed formation which requires roughly a 0.9m frontage per man, and a 'fighting frontage' – the open order formation – which requires three times this amount, about 2.75m in diameter for each fighter. The extra space allowed the soldier to fully exploit his fighting technique of throwing two pila, and then use his short Spanish-style sword for close-quarter battle, dodging and weaving back and forth, stabbing, thrusting and blocking attacks on his person – all the while keeping an eye out for the comrades next to him.

Looking at the battle formation a typical legion would deploy in, we can calculate further. A manipulus had on average a 20-man front that was six-men deep. In close order, the frontage would be roughly 18m across by 5.5m deep. We do know that space was left between the maniples and we can assume that it would be the same length of about 18m when in close order if not wider to allow for expansion to combat. A typical legion without its cavalry wings occupied about 365m in close order. The cavalry of course would require far more space per horseman compared to the foot soldier.

A battle typically opened with light infantry skirmishing. Then, probably at the moment when the enemy infantry closed in, the velites withdrew between the maniples. Some scholars argue that since the maniples were divided into two sub-units (the centuriae), the posterior unit of 60 men would shift over to plug the holes between the maniples; in effect, the 20-man front now extended into a 40-man front three ranks deep, presenting an uninterrupted front to the enemy.

After this, according to Warry, the two sides would close on each other and then charge. The front ranks of hastati would throw their light pila, quickly followed by their heavy pila, before drawing swords. The battle – a succession of furious combats with both sides drawing apart to recover – might go on for several hours. The maniples of hastati would withdraw in close order, to reform behind the triarii, while the principes move up in open order and pass through the hastati. The posterior centuriae would deploy to the left of their prior centuriae, and then the principes would manoeuvre to within charging distance exposing the tired enemy to a fresh foe and another fierce charge. If the principes became exhausted, their place would be taken by a line of triarii spearmen (Warry 1980, p. 111).

To be able to execute these kind of tactical shifts would require several less intense phases during a battle, which is possible, given that no man can swing his weapon and shield indefinitely. It seems more reasonable to argue

The Roman legion in open order.

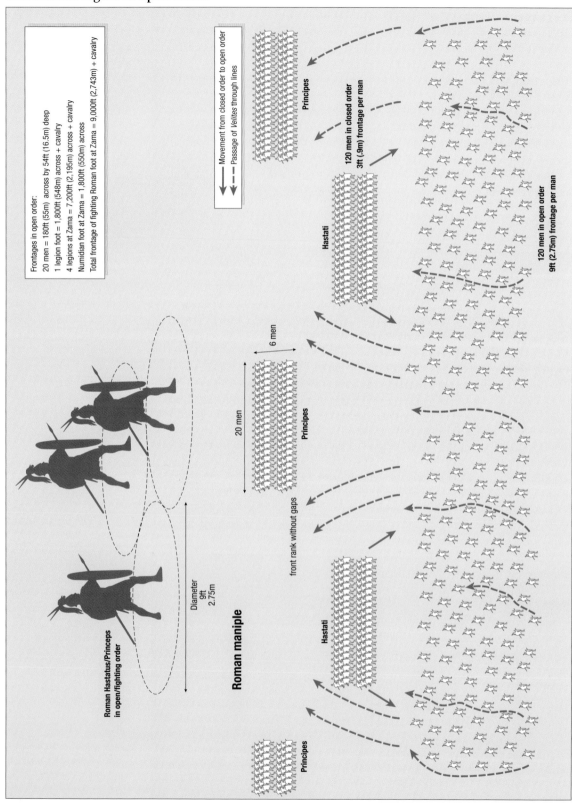

Frontages in open order:
20 men = 180ft (55m) across by 54ft (16.5m) deep
1 legion foot = 1,800ft (548m) across + cavalry
4 legions at Zama = 7,200ft (2,195m) across + cavalry
Numidian foot at Zama = 1,800ft (550m) across
Total frontage of fighting Roman foot at Zama = 9,000ft (2,743m) + cavalry

→ Movement from closed order to open order
⇢ Passage of *Velites* through lines

Principes

120 men in closed order
3ft (.9m) frontage per man

Hastati

120 men in open order
9ft (2.75m) frontage per man

6 men

20 men

Principes

front rank without gaps

Hastati

Principes

Roman Hastatus/Princeps
in open/fighting order

Diameter
9ft
2.75m

Roman maniple

that, once deployed onto the field of battle, the maniples assumed a more lax formation, with greater space for each infantryman, thus extending the battle lines significantly.

Since we know that the fighting man required a 2.75m diameter and we know for certain that it is nearly impossible to maintain straight-line formation, we come to an interesting interpretation of the open order formation by J. E. Lendon. He depicts the hastati and principes assembled in loose formation whereas the triarii present an orderly phalanx, which makes sense, since they were armed with spears and probably would advance or cover their comrades in a more classical hoplite manner – shield to shield, spears levelled (Lendon 2001, p. 181).

Based on Polybius's measurements, one can deduce that the Roman legions may have started with closed order of 0.9m per man, and as they filed onto the plain to seek battle deployed into an open order allowing them to use their weapons most efficiently. Walbank also argues for 1.8m of space between

The Ksour-Essef cuirass, on display at the Bardo National Museum in Tunis. This bronze masterpiece was probably manufactured in Italy around 300 BC. It was discovered in 1910 at Ksour-Essef, Tunisia, in a sarcophagus of cypress wood at a burial site. The head represents the goddess Minerva. (Alexander Van Loon)

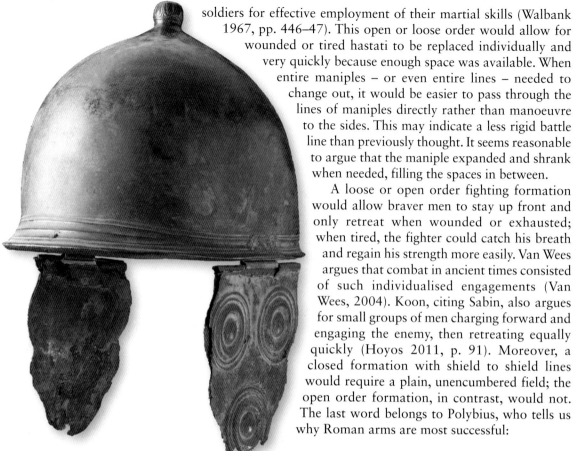

soldiers for effective employment of their martial skills (Walbank 1967, pp. 446–47). This open or loose order would allow for wounded or tired hastati to be replaced individually and very quickly because enough space was available. When entire maniples – or even entire lines – needed to change out, it would be easier to pass through the lines of maniples directly rather than manoeuvre to the sides. This may indicate a less rigid battle line than previously thought. It seems reasonable to argue that the maniple expanded and shrank when needed, filling the spaces in between.

A loose or open order fighting formation would allow braver men to stay up front and only retreat when wounded or exhausted; when tired, the fighter could catch his breath and regain his strength more easily. Van Wees argues that combat in ancient times consisted of such individualised engagements (Van Wees, 2004). Koon, citing Sabin, also argues for small groups of men charging forward and engaging the enemy, then retreating equally quickly (Hoyos 2011, p. 91). Moreover, a closed formation with shield to shield lines would require a plain, unencumbered field; the open order formation, in contrast, would not. The last word belongs to Polybius, who tells us why Roman arms are most successful:

An excellent example of a 3rd century BC Etruscan bronze helmet with cheek guards, of triple disk design. This example is on display at the Los Angeles County Museum of Art, USA.

> Every Roman soldier, once he is armed and sets about his business, can adapt himself equally well to every place and time and can meet attack from every quarter. He is likewise equally prepared and equally in condition whether he has to fight together with the whole army or with a part of it or in maniples or singly. So since in all particulars the Romans are much more serviceable, Roman plans are much more apt to result in success than those of others. (Polybius 18.31.10–12)

THE CARTHAGINIAN ARMY AT ZAMA

The army which nearly brought Rome to its knees had been forged on the anvil of war in Spain by Hannibal. It was there that the Carthaginian leaders perfected numerous tactical manoeuvres and fine-tuned the command and control structure of a great many different peoples (each with their own unique language and military skills). However, unlike their Roman counterparts, little information survives regarding their make up, fighting techniques and tactical dispositions. Peter Connolly states that the success of the Hannibalic army is 'a tribute to the Carthaginian system' where 'each native group fought in its own way and had to be used to its best advantage'.

Hannibal's relationship with his troops was remarkable. In spite of their mixed backgrounds, they stayed with him for 15 years with never the whisper of a mutiny. Polybius seeks to answer the question as to why the Romans were initially defeated by Hannibal's forces in the Second Punic War, before eventually gaining the upper hand:

> It was not owing to their arms or their tactics, but to the skill and genius of Hannibal that they met with those defeats ... And my contention is supported by two facts. First, by the conclusion of the war: for as soon as the Romans got a general of ability comparable with that of Hannibal, victory was not long in following their banners. Secondly, Hannibal himself, being dissatisfied with the original arms of his men, and having immediately after his first victory furnished his troops with the arms of the Romans, continued to employ them thenceforth to the end. (Polybius 18.28–32)

Hannibal's army is interesting for it included a large number of elephants; we know he had none towards the latter stages of his campaigns in

Hannibal crossing the Alps – a somewhat fantastical 19th-century German engraving, but one that gives a good sense of the multicultural nature of Hannibal's forces.

This engraving by Albert Charpentier (1878–1916) of Hannibal crossing the Alps gives a sense of the logistics required to support such a large army. His men are struggling to move an ox-drawn cart through the snow.

Italy. If we are to believe Polybius, there were more than 80 of them at Zama, followed by three lines of infantry equal in size, 12,000 per rank. Mercenaries, some of them veterans of the Italian campaigns under Mago, comprising Ligurians, Celts, Balearian slingers and Mauri were placed in the first line, followed by Liby-Phoenicians or, as Polybius identifies them, Libyans and Carthaginians. The final line, held at a greater distance from the enemy than the two ahead of it, consisted of Hannibal's veterans. There were also two distinct cavalry groups present at Zama. One was small, perhaps around 2,000 strong, consisting of Numidians under their leader Tychaeus, who had sworn loyalty to Hannibal. The other cavalry detachment was probably composed of Carthaginians, Bruttians from Italy and Iberians; it was smaller in number than the Roman and allied cavalry.

The combined paper strength of the Carthaginian–Numidian army (at the upper end) totalled 80 or more elephants, 36,000 foot and between 3,600 and 4,000 mounted troops (Lazenby 1998, pp. 220–21).

The Carthaginians

Prior to the Second Punic War, a key formation in the Carthaginian army comprised the 'Sacred Band', a phalanx of 2,500 citizen soldiers supposedly trained from an early age and consisting of the cream of Carthage's youth. The band was annihilated at the battle of the Krimissus in 341 BC in Sicily during one of the Greco-Carthaginian wars. Thereafter the Carthaginian citizens provided a defensive force primarily against Agathocles, the Sicilian king, and finally against Scipio during the Second Punic War. Unable to sustain losses to its own citizenry, Carthage hired Libyans and other mercenaries to bear the brunt of the fighting. These armies were officered by Carthaginians.

At Zama, the Carthaginian soldiers probably wore a variety of helmets and body armour, from older-style Greek linen and bronze cuirasses to various chest protectors worn by other races, and perhaps even the heavier ring mail favoured by Celtic nobility and wealthier soldiers. Their shields may have comprised Greek-style round shields and an assortment of larger, body-covering oval shields akin to those of the Celts and Italian peoples.

The battle of Himera in 480 BC. Gelon, King of Syracuse, defeated Hamilcar the Magonid, thereby crippling Carthage's power in Sicily for many decades. This was one of many battles – and perhaps the most important of them – during the Greco-Carthaginian wars between 600 and 265 BC.

In this work by Henri Paul Motte (1846–1922), a French artist specialising in historical illustrations, we see Hannibal's army fighting off an ambush in a gorge on its passage across the Alps.

The principal weapon was probably still the spear with a bronze butt-spike and a secondary weapon, which was either provided by the city and thus manufactured wholesale or purchased based on personal choice. The swords were probably based on the prevailing trends of the time such as the Spanish falcata or the Greek kopis.

The cavalry Hannibal fielded on one wing was solely Carthaginian according to our sources, but included a few veteran horsemen from Italy; we are told that Hannibal was unable to transport his horses to North Africa. The Carthaginian cavalry was probably heavier in nature to that of the Numidian light cavalry, but must have been able to fight not only swift Numidian-type horsemen but also the more heavily equipped Romans. Thus the Carthaginian cavalry group could have worn both light and heavy armour. We can assume the cavalry was composed of the elite citizenry.

In 1842 the German historical painter Alfred Rethel (1816–59) began a series of works depicting Hannibal's crossing of the Alps. On the right side of this image we can see the word Sagunt – the town Hannibal sacked prior to invading Italy.

Elephants

The elephants primarily used by the Carthaginian armies were of the now extinct smaller African kind. They stood between 2m and 2.5m tall. These elephants were taken from the now long-vanished forests of Numidia. Their primary use was to terrify the uninitiated, man and horse, and they did carry a single rider each known as a mahout, who was armed with a javelin. Each elephant may well have carried an additional soldier armed with javelins riding on its back. In general, the Carthaginian elephants deployed at Zama did not carry infantry in howdahs on their backs.

Carthage learnt the use of elephants from fighting in Sicily against Pyrrhus of Epirus between 278 and 276 BC as Konstantin Nossov points out:

> Having experienced the effect of this new weapon, Carthage quickly realised that she, too, could acquire it, as African forest elephants inhabited North Africa in great numbers. It was much easier to hire professionals to catch this variety of elephants rather than importing elephants from India. Soon Carthage had the most powerful elephant corps in the Mediterranean world, with stables housing up to 300 elephants located in the capital. Elephants now replaced chariots as the Carthaginians' main striking power. (Nossov 2008, p. 26)

Professor F. E. Adcock describes the less than useful performances of elephants in ancient combat:

> In fact, if all the battles in which they appear are examined, they are found more often involved in defeat than in the forefront of success. And it may be appropriate to observe that when skillfully assailed they may go into reverse, as in attack on a Roman army in Sicily in the First Punic War. And they were prone to panic and might trample down their own men, as at Magnesia. They were, indeed, chancy combatants and needed to be very skillfully controlled by their drivers. (Adcock 1957, pp. 55–56)

Another vivid scene by Alfred Rethel, depicting the hardships Hannibal's army experienced crossing not only the Alps but also the Pyrenees.

Celts and Spaniards

These warriors were heavily recruited during Hannibal's campaign in Italy. They were formidable mercenaries wielding long swords for slashing and spears, and carried a large rectangular shield – not as well manufactured as the scutum but serviceable for the infantry. Celtic warfare was steeped in individual combat and their massive swords required sufficient space to wield a wide sweep or to slash and stab. Hannibal allowed the Celts throughout the war to fight in their own distinctive manner, and by the time of Zama some of these mercenaries may have been equipped with non-traditional items. Although the Celts provided large numbers of infantry and cavalry for Hannibal, no evidence exists for the presence of Celtic cavalry at Zama; if they were present, then arguably it would be in small numbers. Cavalry was often, but not exclusively, composed of nobles who would wear ring mail and carried round shields.

We also lack evidence for a Spanish contingent fighting at Zama, except for a few cavalry troops. However, it is quite possible that some Spaniards were present. Hannibal had previously used Spaniards in separate formations, but by the time of Zama any surviving Spaniards loyally serving with him may have become less distinctive in arms and armour and more likely than not would have fought alongside their comrades.

The Spaniards, like the Celts and Gauls, traditionally provided cavalry and infantry, both light and line, to Hannibal. The infantry had similar shields to the Celts called scutarii, although some of their lighter troops carried smaller, more rounded ones called caetrati which measured 30–60cm in diameter. Spanish infantry carried a variety of spears, including a form that some scholars believe the Roman pilum was based upon. However, their primary weapon was a falcata, which featured a strong blade with a slight curve. This was adapted and modified by the Romans, evolving as the gladius.

Polybius says that Spanish troops were identified by their national dress, which was white with a border of purple. Personal body armour was limited for Spanish troops, and most of them fought with little or any of this. Instead, they wore large leather belts, small disks to protect the chest akin to pectorals and non-metal helmets supposedly made of sinew or a combination of leather with sinew. No doubt, after many years of hard campaigning throughout the Mediterranean they wore some kind of armour, from disks, to cuirasses of various material, to ring mail, and by the time of Zama – if present – may have been all but indistinguishable from the Bruttians. One can easily imagine veteran Celtic and Spanish warriors wearing a variety of gear that included captured hastati and principes chest plates as well as Celtic ring mail.

A falcata sword, the primary weapon of the Spanish infantryman and probably used as a model for the Roman gladius. (Luis García)

A relief showing a Spanish soldier with a large shield and a falcata sword, from the National Archaeological Museum of Spain, Madrid. Note the helmet, which may have been made of sinew and leather.

Bruttians, Ligurians and Balearians

The Bruttians were an Oscan people from southern Italy and served with Hannibal in his Italian campaigns. Traditionally they fought with spears but were equipped in a very similar fashion to the Romans. They wore square chest plates, triple-disk armour, muscled cuirasses and perhaps even helmets of the Greek colonies associated with southern Italy. In addition, they carried large shields, wore a single greave and were armed with sturdy swords, making for a formidable infantry opponent. In the later stages of the Second Punic War, and by the time the battle of Zama took place in North Africa, they had no doubt incorporated equipment from many other peoples into their panoply.

The Ligurians were primarily light infantry skirmishers. Dwelling in north-west Italy and south-eastern France, they had contact with Celts and Italians. They may have carried Celtic-type shields and a variety of daggers, as well as short and long swords. Their clothing was basic, probably items most commonly associated with shepherds such as cloaks and furs. Their primary function within Hannibal's armies was as skirmishers, and to that end they carried javelins and could also fight with sword and shield when the situation required. One can assume that wealthier Ligurians could afford to purchase better armour and veteran fighters may very well have adapted captured equipment to their own needs.

The Balearians were famous slingers who were capable of accurate and deadly fire with their stone projectiles. They carried a variety of slings for different types of stones and use at different ranges. Some may have carried small shields to parry incoming missile attacks. Clearly their role was to harass enemy skirmishers.

Heinrich Leutemann (1824–1905) was a German artist and book illustrator from Leipzig. This 1866 print of Leutemann's shows the Carthaginian crossing of the Alps. As Hannibal and his men come under attack from above, a driver (bottom right) savagely beats his horse onwards, while in the far distance an elephant falls to its death from the treacherous path.

The Liby-Phoenicians and Berber tribes

The complex history of the native nomadic and semi-nomadic peoples who lived in North Africa receives, in ancient sources, scant attention until the advent of the Second Punic War; even then the tribes are mostly lumped into the Berber grouping.

We can assume that the Liby-Phoenicians (which Livy merely designates as 'Africans') comprised a intermixing of varying degrees of Phoenician Carthaginians and Libyan Berbers. The Libyans were a subject people to the Carthaginians and, as noted previously, at times rebelled against their masters. Nonetheless they provided the core of the Carthaginian army aside from mercenaries, as both cavalry and infantry. By the time of Zama we can assume the Libyan infantry were equipped as regular line troops, with arms and armour identical to that of the Carthaginians. Libyans and Liby-Phoenicians had fought in every theatre of the war, and the veterans who fought in Italy dressed themselves in Roman armour. Their equipment consisted of large oval or oblong shields, short cut-and-thrust swords and throwing spears, and possibly fighting spears with butt-spikes. An interesting note is provided by Livy when commenting on the battle of the Great Plains. He details the Roman double envelopment manoeuvre against raw recruits of the Liby-Phoenicians, whom he describes as a 'half-armed mob of peasants hastily collected from the fields' (Livy 30.28.4). It may thus be that a large number of the Liby-Phoenicians were poorly equipped and ill-suited to battle against professional soldiers.

The Mauri were the subjects of a Berber tribal kingdom in the far west in present-day Morocco. Trade was already well established with Carthage by the 3rd century BC and we know that their king at the time of the Second Punic War was Baga. The Mauri also had close contact with the Numidians. The Mauri were employed as mercenaries and may very well have been used primarily as archers and skirmishers. They were probably lightly armed with javelins or spears and bore round shields, and most likely fought alongside Balearian slingers at Zama.

A further Berber tribe comprised the Numidians, who occupied what is now Algeria and part of Tunisia in North Africa. The Numidians were made up of two tribal groups, the Masaesylii in the west and the Massylii in the east. The Numidian light cavalry was considered the finest of its time. It fought as light cavalry, primarily harassing the enemy on sturdy, smaller horses. The latter were ridden bareback with only a single rein for control. The Numdians wore simple tunics, possibly sheepskin cloaks or other animal hides, and carried javelins. Some had small round shields. As a nomadic or semi-nomadic people they were accustomed to the rigours of the outdoors and were excellent scouts. In combat they could close quickly, hurl a shower of javelins and retreat, repeating this tactic until out of javelins. We know that Numidians also provided infantry and some of these fought alongside their mounted comrades in the role of light and line infantry in formation. We also know that the Romans had trained Syphax's men, and Masinissa's Numidians may also have received some training and equipment.

To the south of the Numidians and Mauri dwelled the battle-hardened Berber tribe of the Gaetuli, who inhabited the large desert region south of the Atlas Mountains bordering the Sahara.

Alfred Rethel's drawing shows the aftermath of a fall. An elephant's crushed body reveals a broken tusk while men are impaled on branches. A lone wolf lurks in the background.

ORDER OF BATTLE AT ZAMA

CARTHAGINIAN AND ALLIED (HANNIBAL BARCA)
The first line and elephants (c.10,000–12,000)

A large number of elephants were lined up in front of Hannibal's infantry. The elephants were small and without towers.

Alongside the elephants were skirmishers from Hannibal's first line composed of light and line infantry mercenaries. Their purpose was to protect the elephants against velites and to exploit any gaps the elephants might create. The rest of the first rank would be close by to join the penetration and provide protection for the skirmishers once the hastati advanced and clashed with the spearmen of the first line.

The second line (c.10,000–12,000)

Composed of Carthaginian citizen volunteers and conscripts, as well as Liby-Phoenician spearmen.

The third line (c.8,000)

The 'old guard' comprised Bruttian swordsmen and other veteran campaigners knowledgeable in the martial arts of the Roman soldier.

The left cavalry wing (Tychaeus)

2,000 Numidian horsemen.

The right cavalry wing

Between 1,600 and 2,000 Carthaginian horse.

ROMAN AND ALLIED (PUBLIUS CORNELIUS SCIPIO)
Roman legions V and VI

These legions, together with two allied ones, occupied the centre of the Roman line.

Velites to the front as skirmishers (c.4,800). Their primary purpose was to eliminate the elephant threat.

Hastati in the front line (c.4,800).

Principes in the second line (c.4,800). Possibly used to reinforce the front line and as a manouevre element when required.

Triarii in the third line (c.2,400). The last line of defence or a manouevre element during the climax of the battle.

Numidian infantry (c.6,000)

The Numidian light and line infantry was positioned to the right of the legions. Some may have supported the cavalry. Appian tells us they suffered more casualties (4,000, including 2,500 dead) than the Romans.

Numidian cavalry (Masinissa)

The Numidian cavalry under Masinissa anchored the far right of the Roman army, with 4,000–6,000 horsemen.

Roman and allied cavalry (Laelius)

Laelius's cavalry was on the far right (1,600–2,400 horsemen). They may have been supported by 1,600 Numidians led by Prince Dacamas.

THE BATTLE OF ZAMA

THE LOCATION

The location of the battle of Zama has not yet been identified. No archaeological evidence exists to confirm any of the proposed sites, and conflicting ancient sources only add to the confusion. Livy's comments on the location of the battle are as follows:

> Scipio took up his position not far from the city of Naraggara on ground which, in addition to other advantages, afforded a supply of water within range of missiles from the Roman lines. Hannibal selected some rising ground about four miles [6.5km] away, a safe and advantageous position, except that water had to be obtained from a distance. A spot was selected [for the meeting between Hannibal and Scipio] midway between the camps, which, to prevent any possibility of treachery, afforded a view on all sides. (Livy 30.29)

The historians Gilbert and Colette Picard identify the location as not far from 'Zama, the Massylian capital, probably in the plain of Siliana, where the road from Hadrumetum (Sousse) to Sicca (El Kef) crossed at a road

J. M. W. Turner's 1815 painting *Dido building Carthage*, also known as *The Rise of the Carthaginian Empire*. The original resides in the National Gallery, London. Turner's work captures a sense of the glory and romance of Carthage in its heyday, and is one of several works he painted on this subject.

leading directly from Carthage along the valley of Wadi Miliana' (Picard and Picard 1987, p. 265). Lazenby (1998, p. 218) believes it to have been fought near the town of El Kef (ancient Sicca Veneria), and places Seba Biar about 13km west of Zanfour. He writes that the battle was fought some distance from there, however, and about 5km from Scipio's camp. The location of Scipio's encampment is the key to placing the battlefield. Lazenby believes Naraggara is too hilly and that Livy may have assimilated Naraggara and Margaron. However, the plain of Draa el Meinan (or Metnam), just south of the modern road P5 from Sidi Youssef to El Kef – about 27km from Sidi Youssef, and near the juncture with the road from Kasserine to El Kef – was suitable for accommodating large armies, in his view (Lazenby 1998, p. 218).

Hoyos arrives at a different conclusion:

> [Hannibal's] march went by Zama, one of several towns so named in the hinterland: probably the one later called Zama Regia (today a site called Seba Biar, fifteen miles south-east of El Kef). Zama, though only an encampment on the march, gave its name to the battle through a careless mistake by his biographer Nepos two centuries later. (Hoyos 2008, p. 107)

The German historian Johannes Kromayer and Austrian artillery officer Georg Veith expended considerable energy examining the various theories regarding the location of the battlefield. Their conclusion – accepted by many modern scholars – is that Scipio established his camp, or position, near Margaron (Henchir el Chemmam) and more precisely in the direction of the Sicca Veneria–Naraggara route west towards Numidia. Hannibal, they conclude, left Hadrumetum and force-marched his army either via Sidi Abd el Djedidi or Kairouan until he reached Zama (Seba Biar). Here, they argue, Hannibal sent out reconnoitring parties and subsequently moved towards Scipio's consular army. The two armies probably faced one another across the plain of Draa el Meinan. Scipio's camp was therefore located on the hill called Koudiat el Beheima, which also had access to water from the stream called Qued Ras el Ogla. Hannibal established his camp about 5.5km away on the waterless hill known as Koudiat Bongrine (Kromayer and Veith 1903, p. 38).

Fyodor Bronnikov (1827–1902) painted this powerful scene in 1878 in the Cursed Field, Rome where slaves were crucified. The original is held in the Tretyakov Gallery, Moscow, Russia. Crucifixion was the fate that awaited some of the captured Roman deserters in the wake of the battle of Zama.

THE MEETING OF SCIPIO AND HANNIBAL

Hannibal's army marched five days west from Hadrumetum and established an encampment. From there he sent out Numidian scouting parties, one of which was captured but allowed to enter the Roman camp and return to Hannibal unmolested reporting everything its members had seen. Polybius tells us that Scipio's act of kindness towards the spies intrigued Hannibal enough to seek out a meeting between the two commanders:

> On their return Hannibal was so much struck with admiration of Scipio's magnanimity and daring, that he conceived, curiously enough, a strong desire to meet him and converse with him. Having decided on this he sent a herald saying that he desired to discuss the whole situation with him, and Scipio, on receiving the herald's message, assented to the request and said he would send to Hannibal fixing a place and hour for the interview. (Polybius 15.5.5–11)

Some scholars believe that Scipio allowed the scouts to report back to Hannibal because Masinissa's large Numidian force had not yet joined them. Scipio was deceiving Hannibal.

Meanwhile Scipio was reinforced by Masinissa and his growing army of Numidians. Together they marched toward Naraggara where they established a marching camp at a location which afforded them access to water. There is no doubt that any captured Carthaginian spies at this time would have been executed, for Scipio would not have wanted Hannibal to know the size of the Roman army which now included 10,000–12,000 Numidians and perhaps a third of the Roman army that had brought about Syphax's downfall. Yet, Hannibal did possess some of the best Numidian horsemen and surely they must have conducted numerous reconnaissance missions and discovered the presence of the large Numidian contingent.

In any event, it is from this fortified marching camp that Scipio agreed to the meeting with Hannibal whose army was encamped roughly 5–6km away on a hill (according to Kromayer and Veith) which lacked a source of water. Those anxious to paint a flattering picture of Scipio argue that even in this – access to water – Scipio was the winner. Polybius informs us that the Carthaginians encamped on a hill 'but was rather too far away from water, so that [Hannibal's] men suffered much hardship from this disadvantage'

An atmospheric depiction by an unknown artist of the meeting of Hannibal and Scipio on the plain of Draa el Meinan the day before the battle of Zama.

(Polybius 15.6.3). Hannibal was aware of Masinissa's cavalry's range and abilities and most likely decided to site his camp in a safe location rather than in one where water was more accessible. Perhaps too, Hannibal had in his mind the nighttime attack by the Romano-Numidian force a year earlier. The two camps overlooked the plain of Draa el Meinan (or Metnan).

The meeting between the two legendary commanders was surely an exception to the rule, if indeed it occurred. But let us assume it did, for our most reliable source, Polybius, mentions it in detail. Hannibal, who supposedly had asked for the meeting, understood that he had failed although he had tested Rome to the limit for two decades. Perhaps Hannibal sought peace, or he may have thought his enemy to be more reasonable than predicted – after all, he had released his scouts. It is highly unlikely that Hannibal thought the Romans would show clemency, and even if – in the unlikeliest of circumstances – Scipio were to agree to a less than harsh peace, Hannibal surely knew that the true power of diplomatic agreements and approval lay with the Roman senate and not with the field commander of the consular army – and the senate would surely not grant leniency. Nonetheless, any peace treaty would allow Carthage a return to mercantile trade and might check Masinissa's territorial ambitions. Even victory in battle for Hannibal would not ensure permanent peace, only a temporary respite.

Perhaps Hannibal was curious to know more about one of Rome's greatest commanders, a commander who had lost his father and uncle battling the Carthaginians. Hannibal may have sensed a kindred spirit of a young man driven against his sworn enemy: there was a lot of Hannibal in Scipio. Perhaps Hannibal, the older, more veteran commander, could gauge Scipio the man, and even intimidate him far from his homeland.

What would have prompted Scipio to seek out Hannibal in person? Was it admiration? Curiosity to see the greatest commander of the times, the man who had terrorised Rome? The man who had single-handedly destroyed a generation of Rome's best and brightest and killed tremendous numbers of citizens? Perhaps Scipio wanted to show Hannibal that he was not to be intimidated by the man or the legend, and to prove that he, Scipio, was no ordinary commander but one who would take on every opponent and battle head on and win it because he too was extraordinary? In fact, had he not learnt from the Carthaginians themselves and incorporated their tactics into the best fighting army of the world? Publius Cornelius Scipio may well have reflected that either he or Hannibal would die in the coming days and this meeting was to be either the culmination of a lifetime's work or a bitter end to his own, unfulfilled desire to conquer Rome's greatest enemy.

Polybius's account may have included the self-serving nature of his narrative as a friend and associate of the Cornelian family. Nonetheless, the two commanders and one interpreter each met – Hannibal in his mid-forties and Scipio in his early thirties. Hannibal recounted his accomplishments and his good fortune and asked Scipio to remember that although the Roman had enjoyed good fortune thus far, it could very well turn on him, erasing all the glory Scipio and Rome had won. Moreover, a victory would do little to enhance Rome's status. Hannibal's terms were as follows:

> I propose that all the countries that were formerly a subject of dispute between us, that is Sicily, Sardinia, and Spain, shall belong to Rome and that Carthage shall never make war upon Rome on account of them. Likewise that the other

islands lying between Italy and Africa shall belong to Rome. Such terms of peace would, I am convinced, be most secure for the Carthaginians and most honourable to you and to all the Romans. (Polybius 15.6–9)

Scipio was unmoved by the offer, for reasons that are not made explicit. His reply only tells us, in short, that victors write history:

He said that neither for the war about Sicily, nor for that about Spain, were the Romans responsible, but the Carthaginians were evidently the authors of both, as Hannibal himself was well aware … 'If before the Romans had crossed to Africa you had retired from Italy and then proposed them, I think your expectations would not have been disappointed. But now that you have been forced reluctantly to leave Italy, and that we, having crossed into Africa, are in command of the open country, the situation is manifestly much changed … Either put yourselves and your country at our mercy or fight and conquer us.' (Polybius 15. 6–9)

Polybius concludes his account of the meeting by stating, 'After this conversation, which held out no hopes of reconciliation, the two generals parted from each other.' The die was now cast: the fates of these two daring commanders, their thousands of followers and their homelands would be decided in battle, which probably took place the next day, 19 October 202 BC.

The armies deploy

For the veterans of the battle of Cannae, including Scipio who had fled the field of battle while rescuing his father from certain death, it must have been a bittersweet moment. We can assume Scipio felt sympathetic towards these veterans: they were not cowards on that fateful day in Italy, more the scapegoats – a fate Scipio was also to suffer at a later date.

Some scholars believe that the invading army possibly had greater numbers of light troops than listed previously. Perhaps for the North African campaign Scipio filled the legions beyond their usual numbers as had been done with the legions at Cannae. There is no hard evidence to suggest this kind of increase and armies tend to deploy fewer troops than paper strength. Lazenby dismisses Livy's Roman numbers of 10,000 to 35,000 as incorrect. He argues that the manpower of the Consular Army was 10,000 Roman infantry, 600 Roman cavalry, 16,000 allied infantry and 1,600 allied cavalry, totalling 28,200 (Lazenby, p. 203). Masinissa added an additional 6,000 foot and 4,000–6,000 horsemen, (Lazenby 1998, p. 219). Additionally Dacamas's 1,600 horsemen (mentioned by Appian) ought to be considered. The combined Romano-Numidian army was 32,000 foot and 9,800 horse. We must however remember that even this number should be reduced by

Ancient siege craft, based on Vitruvius. Hannibal's siege of Saguntum took eight months and left him seriously wounded. No doubt Scipio preferred an open battle with Hannibal to a protracted siege of Carthage. (Anne S. K. Brown Military Collection, Brown University Library)

losses from campaigning, disease, retirement due to injuries and desertion. The Roman navy controlled the sea lanes and it might be argued that Scipio's African army received reinforcements. It is still reasonable to assume that at least 30,000 foot and 6,000 cavalry were present for the engagement at Zama.

The Carthaginians are far harder to quantify in detail. However, Polybius states that 20,000 were killed and an equal number were captured, totalling 40,000 – nothing short of annihilation. This does not allow for the fact that Hannibal, after the battle, was able to rally a certain number of survivors including Bruttian and Iberian cavalry. Hannibal's second line and old guard were far smaller than the 12,000 Polybius mentions, as we shall see during the battle.

Scipio needed a plan which would allow his cavalry to accomplish its mission: to drive off the enemy horsemen and return to the battle, avoiding long pursuits, and plunder and strike the pinned-down infantry of the Carthaginians in their backs. He also had to contend with the elephants facing his combined armies. The tactical conceit to Hannibal was the number of elephants deployed as the front line.

Scipio's deployment was unorthodox for a traditional consular army, but he had previously proven the worth of flexibility and his tactical acumen, as had his legions on the battlefields of Spain. Whether his new North African army was as well trained, he would not know until the day of battle. We rely on Polybius's description of their deployment at Zama. Instead of deploying in checkerboard fashion, Scipio formed his men allowing channels in between the maniples. The velites were thrown to the front, followed by the maniples of hastati, principes and triarii all in line, one following the other with spaces in between. These channels were to allow the velites to retreat through the passages 'as far as the rear of the whole army, and those who were overtaken to right or left along the intervals between the lines'. They would also allow the elephants unencumbered passage through the lines all the way to the rear where the skirmishers were then to dispatch any surviving animals. On the left wing he posted his Roman and allied cavalry under his most trusted commander, Laelius, and the Numidians were posted on the far right (Polybius 3.9.7–10).

According to the German historian Hans Delbrück in *Warfare in Antiquity*, Zama was:

> the first battle in the history of the world in which we find echelon tactics significantly and decisively applied in the conduct of the battle as a great, newly discovered principle. In the echelon formation the tactical units are placed one behind the other, far enough apart so that each can move independently, near enough so that they can directly support each other.

In effect, the distances between each of the hastati, principes and triarii maniples had to be large enough to accommodate approximately 40 or so velites, for we do know that velites were attached to the maniples. We can infer that each sub-unit of velites would retreat to its own parent-manipulus, all the while striking at the elephants in the unencumbered lanes to drive them to the rear of the consular army. The distance between the maniples also meant greater flexibility, so if the commander ordered the last two lines to make tactical adjustments during the battle, they would have enough room to manoeuvre.

The one question left unanswered by the ancient sources regards the disposition of the Numidian infantry. We know the Roman battle line was probably anchored on either side by the allied legions, the V Legion on the right and the VI Legion to the left of centre. In effect the two Roman legions formed the centre of the consular army. The Numidians were positioned on the far right and it can be assumed that this included their foot soldiers (Liddell Hart 1992, p. 175). Other scholars have placed part of the 6,000 Numidian foot behind the triarii, presumably to deal with the elephants, whom they would be experienced with. Others, including Kromayer and Veith, have them intermixed with Masinissa's cavalry but do not distinguish them as foot soldiers. Fields notes how the light foot operated alongside cavalry, being 'endowed with remarkable quickness and used to fighting alongside the horsemen and keeping pace with them as they advanced or retreated' (Fields, 2010, p. 100). This, though, would mean that 10,000–12,000 Numidians were intermixed of cavalry and foot, as opposed to the 2,000 Carthaginian loyal light cavalry under Tychaeus. And this would also not account for the 1,600 men of Dacamas nor for the large number of dead Masinissa's troops suffered. Liddell Hart places the Numidian foot immediately to the right of the allied legion with their right flank protected by Masinissa's light horse. Walbank argues that the Numdians fought alongside their mounted comrades.

Lago (2013, p. 60) stipulates 5,000 Numidian foot deployed in front of the 4,800 velites opposing 10,000 of Hannibal's Numidian skirmishers who are ahead of the elephants. He argues that both Hannibal and Scipio sent forward their Numidians to protect their deploying armies. Afterwards Masinissa's skirmishers retired behind the triarii along with the velites. Furthermore, he proposes 8,800 hastati and the same number of principes while the triarii remain at 2,400. The Romano-Numidian cavalry totals 5,500 facing 4,000. On Scipio's left flank he proposes 1,500 Italo-Romans facing 2,000 'African' cavalry, the advantage lying with Hannibal's mounted troops. Additionally, the Carthaginians behind the elephants comprise 12,000 mercenaries, 10,000 Africans and last of all 8,000 veterans. If the Numidian foot did in fact act as skirmishers only, it would be hard to accept Appian's 4,000 wounded and killed.

The elephants used in the Carthaginian deployment pose questions. Polybius says that over 80 elephants were on the field of battle, the most Hannibal ever fielded. We do not know if other elephants had been captured, killed or fled in the two previous battles with the Romano-Numidian army. We might assume that the elephants joined Hannibal when he assembled his army, recruiting men and animals, and as such may very well have been relatively young and untrained. It seems clear that there were some elephants present and that

A Celtic helmet discovered buried in a cave in Agris, France. It dates to c.350 BC and is held in the Musée d'Angoulême. The exquisite decorative detail is of particular note. (Chez Casver)

their purpose was consistent with previous usage (by Xanthippus and by Hannibal in Spain). No matter the actual number, if we are to take Polybius at face value and accept 80 elephants, it means in effect that two elephants faced a front-line manipulus. How could so few cause such problems on the flanks? An enraged or fearful elephant charging an infantry unit could certainly cause a number of casualties; the cavalry component, however, was far more mobile and, in this case, we must assume the Carthaginian horses were accustomed to elephants.

Sometimes the first line of 12,000 mercenaries is discussed as though it were a solid line of infantry, but Delbrück argues for two lines, believing the first line to be skirmishers only (Delbrück 1990, p. 372). Liddell Hart says this first line of three ought not be misconstrued as consisting solely of light troops (Liddell Hart 1992, p. 177). Elephants surely had to have some skirmishers supporting them otherwise they would have been left unprotected and at the mercy of velites and hastati and they probably were an easier target to kill. The first line may have been composed of light infantry as well as line infantry as this front rank consisted of Balearic slingers, Mauri spearmen and archers, as well as Celts and Ligurians (Polybius 15.11.1). However odd this may seem, perhaps the intention of Hannibal was to use the first line to support and exploit the elephant attack, and to do so he needed a flexible front line – skirmishers and infantry capable of tangling with velites and hastati. Perhaps his intention was to simply use the elephants and first rank of mixed troops to grind down the maniples and thus force Scipio to commit his second rankers, the principes, earlier than he preferred, thereby eliminating Scipio's ability to use the second rank as manoeuvre elements. Perhaps the light-armed troops accompanied the elephants, and upon their failure to disrupt the Roman lines, these skirmishers joined the rest of the first rank composed of line infantry as they moved forward to clash with Scipio's hastati maniples.

Were there 12,000 soldiers in the first rank? We know they faced 40 maniples of 120 hastati each, no fewer than 4,800 men. Since each maniple had roughly a 20-man front, there would be 800 hastati to the very front

Carthaginian elephants crossing the Rhone before their ascent into the Alps, by Henri Motte (1878). The elephants shown appear rather large and carry howdahs with armed men in them. The mahout on the right sits atop the elephant's head.

The frontages of the opposing sides at Zama.

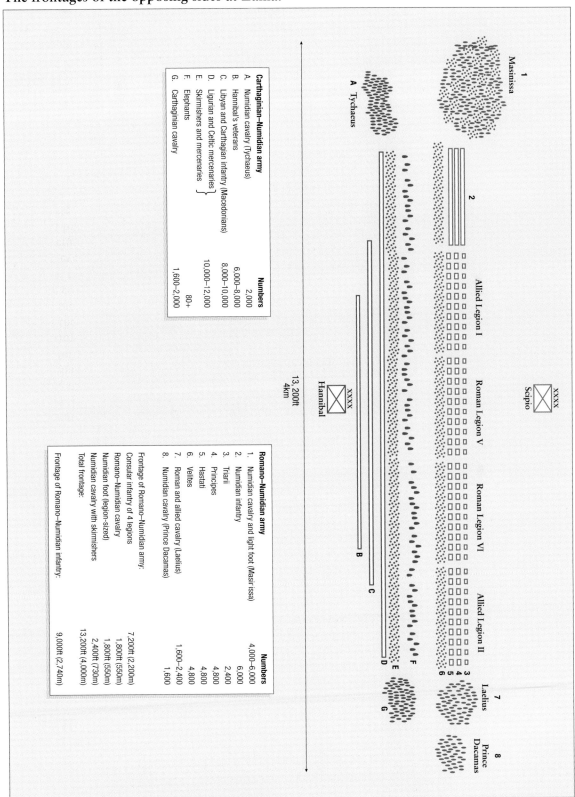

Carthaginian–Numidian army

	Numbers
A. Numidian cavalry (Tychaeus)	2,000
B. Hannibal's veterans	6,000–8,000
C. Libyan and Carthaginian infantry (Macedonians)	8,000–10,000
D. Ligurian and Celtic mercenaries	10,000–12,000
E. Skirmishers and mercenaries	
F. Elephants	80+
G. Carthaginian cavalry	1,600–2,000

Romano–Numidian army

	Numbers
1. Numidian cavalry and light foot (Masinissa)	4,000–6,000
2. Numidian infantry	6,000
3. Triarii	2,400
4. Principes	4,800
5. Hastati	4,800
6. Velites	4,800
7. Roman and allied cavalry (Laelius)	1,600–2,400
8. Numidian cavalry (Prince Dacamas)	1,600

Frontage of Romano–Numidian army:	
Consular infantry of 4 legions	7,200ft (2,200m)
Romano–Numidian cavalry	1,800ft (550m)
Numidian foot (legion-sized)	1,800ft (550m)
Numidian cavalry with skirmishers	2,400ft (730m)
Total frontage:	13,200ft (4,000m)
Frontage of Romano–Numidian infantry:	9,000ft (2,740m)

13,200ft
4km

1 Masinissa
A Tychaeus
Scipio XXXX
Hannibal XXXX
Allied Legion I · Roman Legion V · Roman Legion VI · Allied Legion II
7 Laelius
8 Prince Dacamas

of the fighting, perhaps up to 1,000. Anymore than that and the maniples would become very thin in depth. Hannibal's first rank then, and using less of a combat diameter than the Roman counterpart requiring 2.75m, would probably have a 1,000–1,200-man front, 10–12 men deep, again allowing for fluidity of the skirmishers within their ranks. However, if we add Masinissa's Numidian infantry (a large-size legion) into the mix, the infantry front would be extended and would bring the total to about 10,800 fighters facing 12,000 in Hannibal's first line. The numbers are otherwise hard to justify because one would assume that the combination of elephants and 12,000 of Hannibal's troops would break the first line of the consular army.

In the second rank, featuring the citizens and Liby-Phoenicians, Livy mentions 4,000 Macedonians under Sopater, either phalangites, but more likely swordsmen. Although scholars have cast doubt on their existence at Zama, it is in many ways irrelevant to the battle; since we know Hannibal let his units fight in the manner they were accustomed to, these men either fought as phalangites or spearmen with swords. The second line was also supposedly 12,000 strong. The fighting quality of these men has at times been questioned but, as we shall see, these men were competent enough and difficult to break down easily.

Our ancient sources state that the third and final line of Hannibal's veterans numbered 12,000; this is based on 20,000 soldiers killed and an equal number captured. We know the Roman casualties numbered between 1,500 and 2,500 killed in total and we assume two to three times as many wounded, whereas the Numidians suffered 2,500 killed with 1,500 wounded. How do we explain the ratio of wounded to killed Numidians? This is probably due to their lack of arms and armour, being lightly armed livestock herders, with the exception of their well-armed leaders and elite mercenaries. By the time the final clash occurred, perhaps a third of the casualties had already been inflicted. There is no proof of this other than we know how closely fought the affair was before the final clash. We are told that Hannibal's last line, now filled on its wings with survivors, equalled that of the Roman one. Out of 12,000 hastati, principes and triarii (paper strength) perhaps 9,400–10,400 men capable of fighting matched the length of the Carthaginian line. Hannibal's 'old guard' must have been small, as its flanks were filled with some of the supposed 24,000 men of the first two lines.

The Numidian foot perhaps formed up alongside the Romans, but the ancients tell us nothing about their actual participation other than the actions of the cavalry. If we are to add the Numidian foot, although Lazenby argues against this, we may very well be closer to 12,000 facing Hannibal's last line but again this would still mean the 'old guard' numbered fewer than 12,000 (Lazenby 1998, p. 225). Polybius notes when commenting on the final clash: 'they were nearly equal in numbers as well as in spirit and bravery, and were equally well armed; the contest was for long doubtful, the men falling where they stood out of determination' (Polybius 15.13.6).

Hannibal clearly lacked cavalry. His Carthaginian 1,600–2,000 cavalry was stationed on the right flank and on his left flank he counted on his 2,000 Numidians to do their best against vastly superior numbers. Delbrück estimates the whole of Hannibal's cavalry to have numbered between 2,000 and 3,000 (Delbrück 1990, p. 370). If he is correct, and the Carthaginian cavalry only fielded 1,000 men, then surely Laelius's cavalry – even without the 1,600 Numidians – could have dispatched them without difficulty.

The battle line frontages

The Roman infantry battle line comprised 40 maniples. Each manipulus had a 20-man front and was six ranks deep. A parade-ground formation gave each soldier about 0.9m of space. Thus the average manipulus must have been at least 18m across its front with a similar gap to the side.

However, such rigidity and closed order would not permit the throwing of pila or the individual's ability to wield his scutum and gladius in close-quarter battle. As noted earlier, Polybius tells us that the fighting man in a Roman soldier required a 2.75m diameter to fight effectively, but another consideration is that humans tend to flock together during times of extreme danger. So a 20-man maniple could stretch and constrict like an accordion from 35m to 60m at any given time during hand-to-hand combat. This kind of flexibility allowed them to move in all directions to favour close-quarter sword-fighting after discharging their pila. The majority of soldiers probably did not engage in simultaneous combat; a large number of them were there to morally support the ones who seek out combat. It is not unreasonable to assume that the more aggressive ones would be at the front where the fighting occurred, and when exhausted or wounded would retire, with some of the non-fighters keeping any aggressive enemy fighters at bay as best they could until their exceptional man had recovered and returned to battle or another courageous man stepped into the breach to fight. Instead of the rear sub-unit, the centuria, of 60 men filling the gaps between the maniples, might the maniples have simply moved forward into line and mushroomed into their position? In effect, as the soldiers moved from close order to open order, they simply filled out the spaces to cover their maniple's width including the gaps. Forty maniples even in close order, with maniple-sized spaces in between and on the flanks of the units, equalling 81 maniples in width, had a frontage of not less than 1.5km. An open-order formation may well have pushed this wider as well as forwards.

The cavalry represents a different challenge for the reconstruction. A squadron (turmae) had a ten-man front that was three men deep. There are a great many different breeds of horses and we do know that the Berber tribes rode sturdy and swift pony-sized horses. A Roman or allied cavalryman required space for himself and his horse to fight and wield his spear, avoid a thrust, lift his shield to block or hit someone with it and to draw his secondary weapon, the sword. In close-order formation one can assume the average horseman required just under 2m to adjust for movement and the rider carrying a round shield and spear. In combat, the Roman cavalryman surely needed at least 5m to allow him to manoeuvre his horse and use his weapons effectively. Thus the minimal frontage of a single Roman turma in open-order formation charging at the enemy – and remembering that horses create channels when other horses run at them – would have occupied at the very least 45–60m across and around 20m deep.

Laelius's Roman and allied cavalry wing anchoring the left side had 80 turmae, each with ten riders to the front by three riders deep, assuming paper strength. Assuming also that Laelius deployed his squadrons in three lines akin to the infantry, we come up with about 26 or so turmae per line – nearly 1.2km wide and with a minimum depth of 40m but which could easily have been 90m if not more. Laelius, of course, may have shrunk his frontage by half and stacked his squadrons deeper.

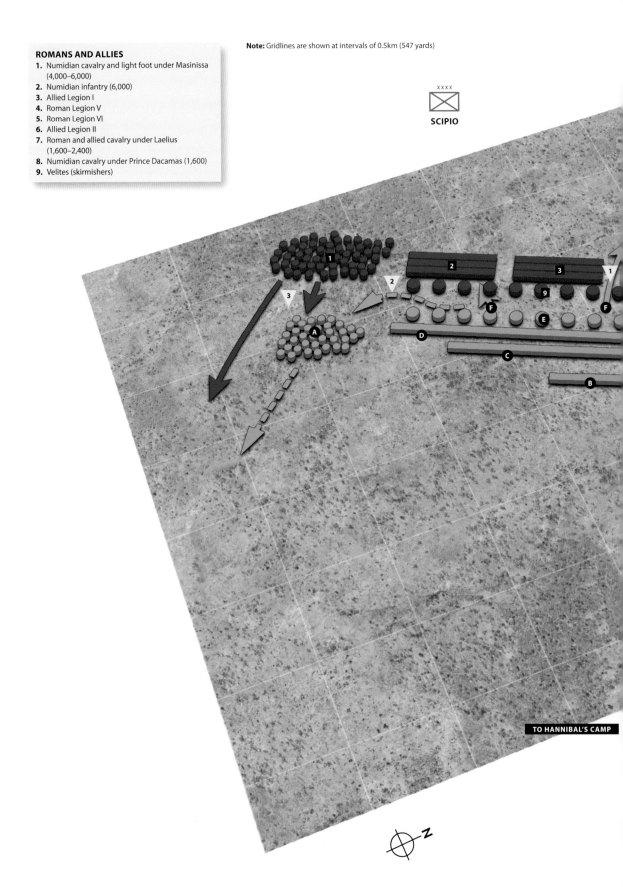

ROMANS AND ALLIES

1. Numidian cavalry and light foot under Masinissa (4,000–6,000)
2. Numidian infantry (6,000)
3. Allied Legion I
4. Roman Legion V
5. Roman Legion VI
6. Allied Legion II
7. Roman and allied cavalry under Laelius (1,600–2,400)
8. Numidian cavalry under Prince Dacamas (1,600)
9. Velites (skirmishers)

Note: Gridlines are shown at intervals of 0.5km (547 yards)

xxxx

SCIPIO

TO HANNIBAL'S CAMP

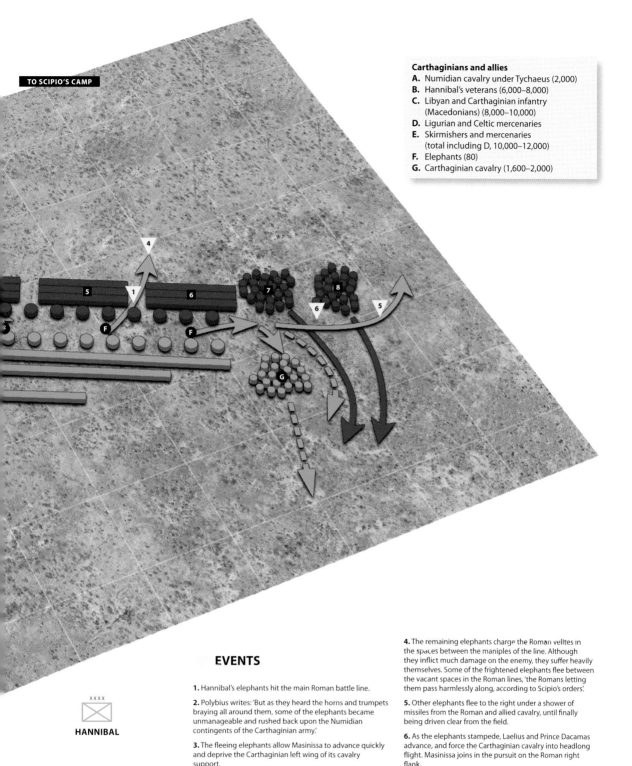

Carthaginians and allies
A. Numidian cavalry under Tychaeus (2,000)
B. Hannibal's veterans (6,000–8,000)
C. Libyan and Carthaginian infantry
(Macedonians) (8,000–10,000)
D. Ligurian and Celtic mercenaries
E. Skirmishers and mercenaries
(total including D, 10,000–12,000)
F. Elephants (80)
G. Carthaginian cavalry (1,600–2,000)

xxxx

HANNIBAL

EVENTS

1. Hannibal's elephants hit the main Roman battle line.

2. Polybius writes: 'But as they heard the horns and trumpets braying all around them, some of the elephants became unmanageable and rushed back upon the Numidian contingents of the Carthaginian army.'

3. The fleeing elephants allow Masinissa to advance quickly and deprive the Carthaginian left wing of its cavalry support.

4. The remaining elephants charge the Roman velites in the spaces between the maniples of the line. Although they inflict much damage on the enemy, they suffer heavily themselves. Some of the frightened elephants flee between the vacant spaces in the Roman lines, 'the Romans letting them pass harmlessly along, according to Scipio's orders'.

5. Other elephants flee to the right under a shower of missiles from the Roman and allied cavalry, until finally being driven clear from the field.

6. As the elephants stampede, Laelius and Prince Dacamas advance, and force the Carthaginian cavalry into headlong flight. Masinissa joins in the pursuit on the Roman right flank.

THE OPENING PHASE OF THE BATTLE: DAYBREAK, 19 OCTOBER

The opposing armies marched out at daybreak ready to give battle. The opposing Numidian cavalry forces engaged first and skirmished for a while before Hannibal ordered the advance of his elephants. Some of the young and untrained elephants became unmanageable, fleeing headlong into the Carthaginian and Numidian cavalry. At this point, Masinissa seized the opportunity to drive off Hannibal's loyal Numidians.

The Roman left composed of open order formation cavalry may very well have stretched to 1.2km, the infantry also in open order at under 2km, leaving us to ascertain the deployment of the cavalry and foot Numidians under Masinissa. His accompanying light infantry was most likely composed of farmers and livestock herders, and we shall assume that the Numidian foot occupied roughly the space of a legion in open order, or 0.5km across. Masinissa's cavalry with 4,000–6,000 troops would require far greater space. Being light cavalrymen, it was a flexible organism, growing, shrinking and moving. It was less rigid in shape, like a giant prickly ball, and its frontage might have presented 500–600 riders. Even if allocated a small combat diameter of at least 3m, they could easily occupy 1.5km but deep in rank allowing for a rotational system of attack in a very fluid, natural manner. If we are to assume the whole of the Numidians fought together, as in foot supporting horse, then their frontage may have been wider and deeper.

THE BATTLE BEGINS

On the day of battle, the opposing armies marched out of their respective camps. The ancient writers tell us nothing about the respective camps and how many men were left behind to guard them. Nor do they mention anything about camp followers, especially for the veterans from Italy. We may presume that, if there were any followers, they had probably remained at Hadrumetum. The sound of horns and trumpets, war cries, horses neighing, elephants trumpeting and soldiers grumbling were no doubt part of it all. Their lines stretched out over several kilometres on the plain of Draa el Meinan.

A plate dated c.1540 from the Fontana workshop, Urbino, Italy, showing Scipio addressing his troops prior to the battle of Zama. (Kunstgewerbemuseum Berlin , inv. nr. K1799)

Both commanders gave speeches. Scipio, according to Polybius, reminded his men that a victory would see Rome gain undisputed command of the known world, and to accomplish this every man had to fight for both themselves and their country:

Keep it before your eyes that if you overcome your enemies, not only will you be unquestioned masters of Africa, but you will gain for yourselves and your country the undisputed command and sovereignty of the rest of the world. But if the result of the battle be otherwise, those of you who have fallen bravely in the fight will lie for ever shrouded in the glory of dying thus for their country, while those who save themselves by flight will spend the remainder of their lives in misery and disgrace. For no place in Africa will be able to afford you safety, and if you fall into the hands of the Carthaginians it is plain enough to anyone who gives due thought to it what fate awaits you. (Polybius 15.10.2–7)

Scipio did not address the Numidians, so far as we know. Hannibal, it appears, did not address all of his men – a departure from what we know of his usual practice of care for his men, sharing their hardships on and off the battlefield. The rest of the army was spoken to by their commanders, who reminded the men that Hannibal would lead them well and to further victory. Hannibal addressed only his veterans directly, some of whom must have served with him since Spain, and he reminded them of the number of the battles they had previously fought against the Romans:

> 'In all these battles,' he said, 'you proved so invincible that you have not left the Romans the smallest hope of ever being able to defeat you. Above all the rest, and apart from your success in innumerable smaller engagements, keep before your eyes the battle of the Trebia fought against the father of the present Roman general, bear in mind the battle of the Trasimene against Flaminius, and that of Cannae against Aemilius, battles with which the action in which we are about to engage is not worthy of comparison either in respect to the numbers of the forces engaged or the courage of the soldiers.' (Polybius 15.11.4–12)

Hannibal then asked his veterans to cast their eyes over the ranks of the enemy, which Polybius states were a fraction of the forces that had faced them in former battles. He urged them not to destroy the glorious record that they had achieved, but, fighting bravely, to 'confirm their reputation for invincibility'.

The plans made by Scipio and his commanders must have included moves to neutralise the elephants, and they must have felt confident in their superiority of cavalry and in their respective commanders Masinissa and Laelius. Scipio had defeated two Carthaginian armies, ravaged the countryside and allowed a portion of his consular army under Laelius to aid Masinissa in his victory over Syphax. The challenge on this day would be presented by Hannibal – for he was an exceptional general, and Scipio had learnt much from the Carthaginian's art of war. At the battle of Baecula in 208 BC he pinned down a well-positioned Hasdrubal and his infantry centre, and launched flanking attacks with his hidden cavalry thereby winning the day – although Hasdrubal was able to retreat with the bulk of his army. At Ilipa in 206 BC he approached with a concave line, refusing battle but pinning down the enemy infantry in the centre, while extending his lines with velites and outflanking Mago's army.

Here, Scipio's plan was similar. The elephants were a nuisance, but he was certain his army could deal with them effectively: there were 40 channels available for the 80 elephants to be driven through. Laelius and Masinissa would drive off the far inferior enemy cavalry while Scipio's hastati maniples pinned down Hannibal's front line. Once Hannibal committed his second and perhaps third line, and Scipio committed his principes to bring relief to his front rank, he would spring his velites and triarii around the flanks to roll up Hannibal's lines. His own cavalry would return in time and completely surround Hannibal, like he had done at Cannae. Of course, no plan survives contact and one must wonder what Scipio thought when he saw the three separate lines deploying right in front of him and Hannibal's veterans far enough back to avoid envelopment. Scipio realised that the clash between the infantry would be hard fought, but the cavalry would be his salvation.

THE OPENING PHASE OF THE BATTLE (PP. 62–63)

This scene shows Hannibal's right flank during the opening phase of the battle, as Hannibal's elephants advance towards the Roman hastati maniples. We can see the gaps (**1**) left in between the maniples to allow for the passage of the elephants. The velites (**2**) have retreated through the maniples or through the same channels. The Roman plan is to allow the elephants to run the gauntlet through to the very rear of the battle lines, where they will be killed or captured by the velites. Some, naturally, will escape.

On the right-hand side, some of the elephants (**3**) have turned away from the Romans (**4**), who are shouting and banging their weapons against their shields; this, together with the sound of horns and trumpets, is intended to frighten the young, untrained elephants. One elephant (**5**) is under attack by javelins thrown by the Roman knights and is turning into the Carthaginian cavalry on the far right flank.

The hastati (**6**) are opening their formation and are extending into the gaps with the neighbouring maniples, thus forming a solid line across the battlefield and extending their close-quarter battle space.

Hannibal's first line (**7**) composed of skirmishers and Mago's mercenaries are moving towards the Roman lines. Mauri, Balearian slingers, archers, Celts, Spaniards and Ligurians are all present in the first rank.

The battle of Zama in an engraving by Cornelis Cort (c.1533–78). Scipio is on horseback (lower right) as Roman soldiers engage Hannibal, who directs his troops from a war elephant in the upper left. The elephants resemble near pre-historic creatures dwarfing the horses and humans they are battling. This image expresses the fear and terror that men and animals unaccustomed to elephants must have felt. (Library of Congress LC-DIG-pga-00039)

Hannibal also held discussions with his subordinate commanders, recalling how they achieved victories against overwhelming odds but also how the Romans had changed their tactics. Reports had reached Hannibal (possibly via veterans) about his brothers' victories and losses, as well as the details of how Carthaginian forces were defeated by Scipio. Hannibal must have known enough about Scipio to realise he would avoid regular battle formation and tactics. Having his centre pinned down might be beneficial to Hannibal if he had sufficient horse, but he could not count on them, and he could not count on the elephants. Hannibal's army was not as well trained or battle hardened as he would have liked but they would do the best they could. His weakness lay in cavalry.

Keeping a battle plan simple was the key. Avoiding encirclement by the enemy infantry could only be accomplished by having a strong reserve, one capable of executing orders quickly and well; stationing this reserve further back was going to offset any of Scipio's tactical manoeuvres. But holding a tactical reserve would only be of little use if the front line collapsed in the face of the enemy's central attacks. To that end Hannibal needed a second line, behind his main front line. This second line would stop the frontal assault of the Romans should they break through the front rank of Mago's mercenaries. His third line would be his manoeuvre element, either to flank the Romans or to punch through them.

The elephants were more of a gamble, and their numbers, according to Delbrück, were 'too small for Hannibal to have based

An exceptional rendering of the martial arts of Romans during battles and skirmishes, by Johann Daniel Herz the Elder (1693–1754). The lack of armour on each soldier, and the space in which they fight, are relevant to the fighting at Zama. (Anne S.K. Brown Military Collection, Brown University Library)

his hopes on them' (Delbrück 1990, p. 371). They might disrupt the legions, but the opposing Numidians were familiar with fighting against elephants, as were the Roman and allied soldiers, so there was no guarantee that the elephants would wreak sufficient havoc. Hannibal also knew that elephants could easily turn and collide with his own forces. It made sense then to safeguard against his own elephants by having two solid lines to carry the brunt of the battle with a third line further back. The added distance to his third rank would allow time for the battlefield to empty itself of the fleeing survivors of the first two ranks, and since Hannibal's 'old guard' was smaller, it would also allow the survivors to join the third rank thereby extending the line. Having a strong veteran last line, like the triarii, would certainly help steady nerves and also allow Hannibal to exploit any weakness exposed in the enemy's formations. Hannibal may very well have intended for his 'old guard' to split in two and outflank the Romans if the possibility occurred, but this might have been made more difficult with the addition of the survivors to his flanks.

To overcome his weakness in cavalry, Hannibal may have planned to lure the enemy horse off the field, thereby giving his infantry enough time to demolish the Roman lines. Perhaps his cavalry commanders were given free rein to either join with the fight and win the battle, or, if they were at risk of losing, to withdraw and present a tempting target for any pursuers – always out of reach, but close enough to pose a threat. Hannibal must have at least realised that his cavalry was not going to encircle and overcome the enemy, as it had previously done.

Polybius (15.12) writes that the opening move of the battle was the cavalry skirmish between the Numidian cavalry. Hannibal then ordered his elephants forward, to charge the enemy. If there were indeed 80 of them, it must have been an awe-inspiring sight. The sounds of men and noises of the animals on the battlefield escalated, but it would have been the horns and trumpets braying all around them and the shouting of the Roman soldiers that overwhelmed some of the elephants, making them unmanageable. Those few elephants turning away in fear towards their left side would have run straight into the Numidian horsemen under Tychaeus who were skirmishing with Masinissa's cavalry. The latter had gained an upper hand, and Tychaeus's men yielded the field and were hotly pursued, leaving Hannibal's left flank now exposed and possibly facing the Numidian foot anchoring the Roman right flank.

Other elephants charged ahead and inflicted many casualties on the velites and hastati before rushing through the open channels. Some clearly crashed into the maniples. Even if the channels were open for the elephants,

A sketch of Roman cavalry charging at skirmishers, attributed to Le Potre (presumably the French engraver Jacques Lepautre or Le Pautre, *c.*1653–84). Note the dense mass formed by the riders. (Anne S. K. Brown Military Collection, Brown University Library)

an enraged and wounded elephant might very well have charged at the source of its pain. A number of elephants were killed and severely wounded during the melee. One can barely imagine the carnage on the battlefield let alone the monstrosity of using elephants for war.

Elephants on the right-hand side of the line deviated to the right where they in turn were showered by javelins by Laelius's cavalry, which seemingly was not engaged with enemy cavalry at the time, until the elephants were driven clear off the field. During this stampede Laelius exploited the situation like the veteran commander he was and forced the Carthaginian cavalry into flight, perhaps rattled by the elephants. The elephants did not turn back into their supporting, first rank; instead, the ones on the flanks veered to the left and right while others charged ahead into the maniples or through the channels left open by the maniples. Surprisingly, Laelius's cavalry was not disturbed by the elephants.

The elephants were controlled by a mahout, or rider, who had a final task to perform if the animal became unmanageable. Livy, writing about the battle of the Metaurus in 207 BC, describes it thus:

> More of the elephants were slain by their own drivers … than by the enemy. These used to have a carpenter's chisel and a mallet. When the beasts began to grow wild and to dash into their own men, the keeper would place the chisel between the ears, precisely at the joint which connects the neck with the head, and would drive it in with all possible force. That had been found to be the quickest means of death in a brute of such size, when they got beyond the hope of control. And the first man to introduce the practice had been Hasdrubal. (Livy 27.49)

The ancient sources say nothing about rampaging elephants at Zama being killed by their mahouts. Perhaps the answer lies in the fact that the riders were exposed to the missiles of the skirmishers and hastati and that many were killed early on as the elephants rampaged. Many of the riderless elephants may have chosen safety and escape over battle. Even if some mahouts were still on top of the elephants, it could not have been easy to pull out the tools required and execute the elephant while dodging javelins at full speed. After all, riding atop an animal that is barely 2m tall does not protect the mahout from a javelin or pilum's reach. Perhaps Polybius was wrong and far fewer than 80 elephants were present at the battle. No matter the numbers, Hannibal knew that elephants were not necessarily a force multiplier. But we do know that the elephants did in fact cause large numbers of caualties among the velites and hastati. In effect the argument must be made that they did accomplish the task that was assigned to them.

Henri-Paul Motte's depiction of the opening phase of the battle of Zama. Although the elephants appear too large and in all likelihood did not carry howdahs, the painting does demonstrate the clash with the velites before they withdrew down the channels left open to them and the pursuing elephants by the maniples.

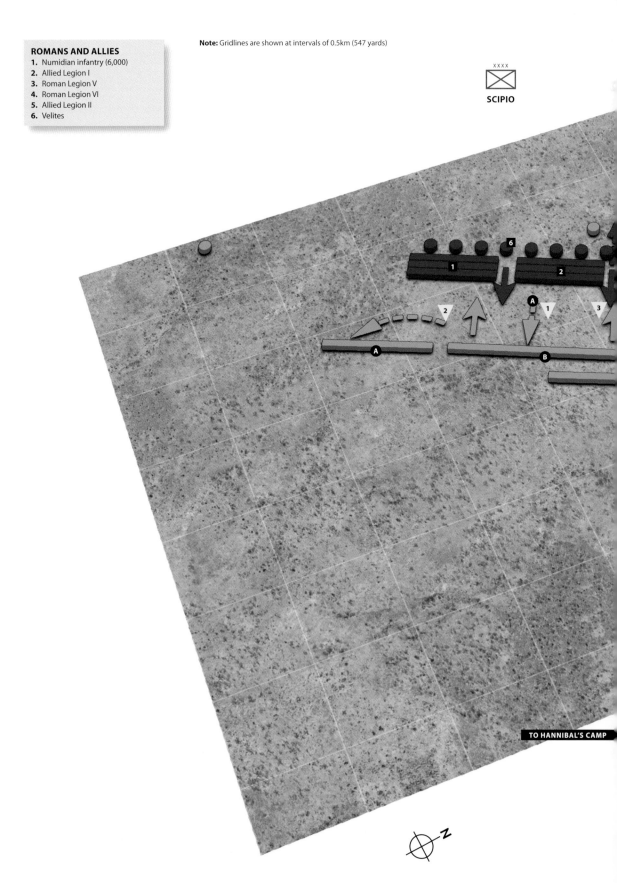

ROMANS AND ALLIES
1. Numidian infantry (6,000)
2. Allied Legion I
3. Roman Legion V
4. Roman Legion VI
5. Allied Legion II
6. Velites

Note: Gridlines are shown at intervals of 0.5km (547 yards)

SCIPIO

TO HANNIBAL'S CAMP

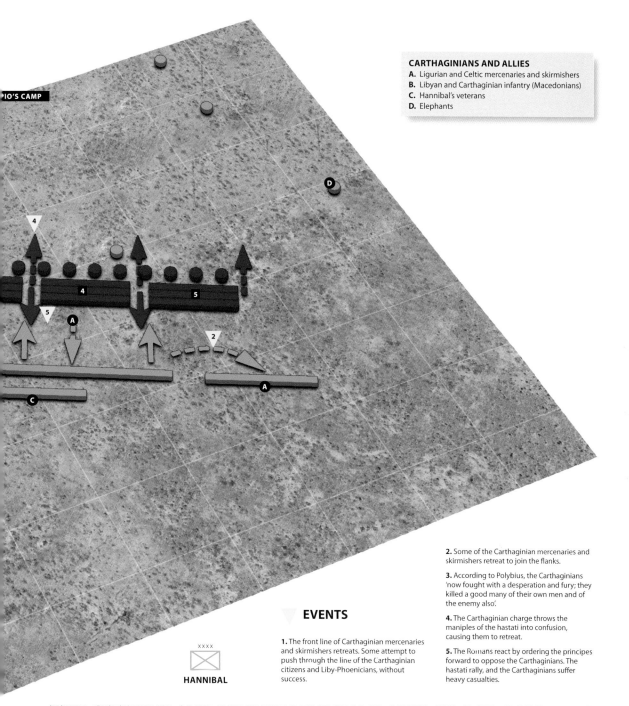

CARTHAGINIANS AND ALLIES
A. Ligurian and Celtic mercenaries and skirmishers
B. Libyan and Carthaginian infantry (Macedonians)
C. Hannibal's veterans
D. Elephants

XXXX

HANNIBAL

EVENTS

1. The front line of Carthaginian mercenaries and skirmishers retreats. Some attempt to push through the line of the Carthaginian citizens and Liby-Phoenicians, without success.

2. Some of the Carthaginian mercenaries and skirmishers retreat to join the flanks.

3. According to Polybius, the Carthaginians 'now fought with a desperation and fury; they killed a good many of their own men and of the enemy also'.

4. The Carthaginian charge throws the maniples of the hastati into confusion, causing them to retreat.

5. The Romans react by ordering the principes forward to oppose the Carthaginians. The hastati rally, and the Carthaginians suffer heavy casualties.

THE CITIZENS AND LIBY-PHOENICIANS ATTACK: MID-MORNING

The elephants had initiated the opening of the battle and now the two lines of Hannibal's infantry advanced. The first line composed of mercenaries fought steadily until they were broken and fled. Some of the survivors remained on the field of battle, joining the flanks of the second line of infantry composed of Carthaginian citizens and Liby-Phoenicians, thereby extending the frontage to match that of the Romans. Hannibal's veterans remained in place and perhaps some survivors joined their flanks at this stage as well. The Carthaginian second line, including mercenaries on the wings, clashed furiously with the hastati and 'their charge threw the maniples of the hastati into confusion; whereupon the officers of the principes caused their lines to advance to oppose them' (Polybius 15.13). The Roman lines were very nearly broken at this stage but managed to drive the Carthaginians back.

THE INFANTRY CLASH

The next phase of the battle comprised the forward movement of the infantry of both sides. We are told that the only line which did not move forward was Hannibal's 'Army of Italy'. This reinforces the notion that Hannibal intended them either as a reserve or as a manoeuvre element during the climax of the battle.

The first rank, probably reconstituted with slingers and archers, came within distance of the hastati and 'charged the enemy, shouting as usual their war cry, and clashing their swords against their shields; while the Carthaginian mercenaries uttered a strange confusion of cries, the effect of which was indescribable' (Polybius 15.12).

By this time, the hastati maniples must have flooded out into open order of battle and filled the channels left for the elephants' passage. The velites were probably dealing with the remaining elephants to the rear of the legions. Each side would throw their javelins or pila, use their spears, draw swords and attempt to kill the other man. Polybius clearly states that this was not a spear fight but one of extreme close-quarter combat between swordsmen. The mercenaries did exceptionally well for they enjoyed a clear superiority, wounding a considerable number of Roman front rankers. It was, as Polybius writes, a trial of strength between the infantry at close quarters.

During the struggle between the hastati and the mercenaries, the second rank of the principes shouted encouragement to their comrades in the first rank – though how anybody fighting in the front could have heard such sounds amidst the noise and carnage around them is difficult to comprehend. Encouragement, however, is often not for the person fighting but for the man supporting the other – anxious to see them victorious. The hastati, relying on their 'steadfastness and excellence of their arms', were gaining ground.

On the other side, the mercenaries received no such support from their comrades in the second line. The citizens and Liby-Phoenicians kept quiet if we are to believe Polybius, and perhaps they cared not for the foreigners fighting for their city – after all, that is what they were being paid to do. Our ancient source lets us believe that that lack of encouragement is the reason why the mercenaries eventually fell back. They may also have given a very good account of themselves, and very likely being exhausted and having suffered killed and wounded, there may well have been good reason for their withdrawal.

Polybius insists the mercenaries retreated because they felt abandoned. Oddly he continues stating that the mercenaries, enraged by this betrayal, battled the second line as they retreated from the advancing Roman lines: in effect, they were so enraged that they fell upon the Carthaginians and began killing them. A reasonable explanation, based on subsequent events, will show this to be false. More probably, the mercenaries retired but instead of being let through

Shallow Bowl with the Triumph of Scipio Africanus, a work by the French enamelist Pierre Nouailher I (active *c*.1660–1717) using painted enamel and gilt on copper. Scipio can be identified by his baton of command, as he leads his troops to victory over the Carthaginians at Zama. (Walters Art Museum)

the Carthaginian ranks as they may have expected, Hannibal had ordered his citizens to maintain their formation and force the surviving mercenaries to stream to their wings, either to add to the frontage, or continue falling back. Either way, the most important aspect was for the citizen second line to remain unbroken and facing the oncoming Roman ranks.

A further question arises: what of the Numidian foot? Surely, if they anchored the allied legion on the far right, they too must have clashed with the mercenaries; the ancient historians, however, remain silent on their contribution. Seemingly the odds were two to one for the mercenaries. Six thousand Numidian foot participating alongside the hastati makes more sense because it seems the Roman second rank was not committed to the attack, just supporting the front rank verbally. Even if we assume the Numidian infantry also had three lines, though it seems less likely, they would have added hundreds if not a thousand to the front line and would have borne some of the fighting. The casualties they suffered were greater than those of the Romans.

The hastati, having dispersed the mercenary front line, now closed with the Carthaginians, who numbered fewer than the 12,000 suggested by some scholars, but whose numbers were increased on the wings by some survivors of the mercenary first line. Upon their clash, the Carthaginians exhibited, not by their own desire but by the situation at hand, a fight with desperation and fury. They killed 'a good many both of their own men and of the enemy also', according to Polybius. He then states Hannibal's second rank of citizens and Liby-Phoenicians charged and threw the maniples of the hastati into confusion:

A 3rd-century BC terracotta oenochoe (wine jug) depicting Tanit, the Carthaginian mother goddess. It was discovered at BeniAsl necropolis, Bizerte, and now resides at the National Bardo Museum, Tunis.

> Thus it came about that their charge threw the maniples of the hastati into confusion; whereupon the officers of the principes caused their lines to advance to oppose them. However, the greater part of the mercenaries and Carthaginians had fallen either by mutual slaughter or by the sword of the hastati. (Polybius 15.13)

Clearly, the Carthaginians had bested Scipio's front rank, depleting it of its fighting strength, for these men had been battling elephants, mercenaries and now Carthaginians and taken casualties in doing so. Seemingly the maniples were ground down, and were nearly broken by the charge of the Carthaginian citizens. At this crucial moment the maniples of the principes moved forwards to oppose the advancing Carthaginians. Polybius does state though that 'the greater part of the mercenaries and Carthaginians had fallen either by mutual slaughter or by the sword of the hastati'. He has us believe that a mere 4,800–6,000 front rankers (8,800 according to Lago) had nearly overcome two lines totalling between 20,000

THE CARTHAGINIANS AND LIBY-PHOENICIANS CLASH WITH THE HASTATI (PP. 72–73)

Hannibal's Carthaginian citizens and Liby-Phoenicians (**1**) – his second line – is pushing the Roman maniples of the hastati (**2**) back. Fighting with spears and swords, the Carthaginians do more than hold their own. They are about to rout the hastati and will be fighting with the principes, who are desperately trying to establish order to the battle line. The principes move through the open-order fighting formation of the hastati. Some of the principes (**3**) are engaging the Carthaginians with their pila before drawing swords. We see a number of Liby-Phoenicians described by Livy as a 'half-armed mob of peasants hastily collected from the fields'. These men (**4**) support the better-armoured men to their front. After a furious struggle the Carthaginians and Liby-Phoenicians retreat to Hannibal's third and final line, composed of 'old guard' veterans.

and 24,000; Lazenby finds this difficult to accept. Only now a further 4,800–6,000 of the second line joined their comrades in the front line. Liddell Hart believes that even the principes began to waver at this point. One can assume that the principes had been committed into the fracas earlier during the clash with the Carthaginians, and that the officers of the principes steadied the line during the confusion. Only if we include the Numidian foot of between 4,000 and 5,000 out of 6,000 – allowing for some to have joined Masinissa's cavalry – can we assume that the principes only joined later on. The battle was a close-fought thing at this point, and the Carthaginian charge bloodied and unsteadied the consular army, forcing Scipio in fact to commit his second line. It is indeed a challenge to believe that so small a force of front-rank maniples could defeat hard-fighting mercenary and citizen lines nearly four times the size. But if we are to accept Polybius's account, then the maniples of the principes restored the balance and thus preserved the Roman army's integrity and survival.

With the approach of Scipio's principes, the surviving Carthaginians and mercenaries retreated and again were greeted by spears, this time by the 'old guard', and forced to flow around Hannibal's last line. Some joined the final rank while others may have fled, perhaps to their camp. Flight into the open country would surely have meant being hunted down by Numidian cavalry, unless of course Hannibal's cavalry was winning the fight, which

A grave stele found near the ancient city of Carthage. Beneath this marker the remains of cremated animals and very young children were discovered.

must still have been taking place off the plain. Nonetheless, at this point both of Hannibal's front two ranks gave a very good account of themselves and nearly routed the hastati, only to be stopped by arrival of the principes. Only then did they retreat, their confidence shattered and exhausted. It may be that they were recalled by Hannibal, who saw the movement of Scipio's second line and wanted to preserve the fighting ability of the Carthaginians and remaining mercenaries. By ordering them back and preserving the unit integrity of the 'old guard' by not allowing passage of line, he added a considerable number to his final rank. Here they could recover, rearm and pause for breath before the final clash.

Polybius's next lines challenge us, for he writes that Scipio ordered the hastati to be recalled from their pursuit, assuming they were chasing down the fleeing mercenaries and Carthaginians, who until the arrival of the maniples from the second rank were actually routing them.

Was Hannibal's rank so far back that there was ample space, time and safety to chase down enemy combatants? In the original formation Hannibal's 'old guard' was placed a stade (180m) behind the second rank. Assuming the mercenaries and Carthaginians charged forwards to clash with the onrushing Romans, this would not appear very likely but perhaps this pursuit only covered a short distance to dispatch the wounded, both on the ground and struggling away. Moreover, the hastati were both exhausted and depleted and perhaps would not have been capable of a pursuit at this point.

At this point, according to Polybius, the two armies were separated by battlefield debris:

> The space between the two armies that still remained in position was full of blood, wounded men, and dead corpses; and thus the rout of the enemy proved an impediment of a perplexing nature to the Roman general. Everything was calculated to make an advance in order difficult – the ground slippery with gore, the corpses lying piled up in bloody heaps, and with the corpses arms flung about in every direction. (Polybius 15.14)

Clearly a desperate struggle had been taking place. The Roman maniples most likely would have withdrawn to reorganise their confused ranks. Hannibal's army must have outflanked Scipio's at this stage and perhaps he was about to order its advance to exploit the confusion within the maniples as they tried to stem the retreat of and potential disorder among the weary hastati. Simultaneously, we can assume that Scipio's velites handled the captured and loose elephants, moved their own wounded and probably dispatched the enemy wounded while the maniples of the principes and triarii manoeuvred through the carnage of the dead and deployed in line with the surviving hastati, assuming that the hastati never broke and merely became disorganised.

Why Hannibal allowed the Roman front line to reorganise remains a mystery. This would have been an excellent time to strike the maniples. Perhaps Hannibal was busy reorganising his own lines of survivors into formations. Surely Hannibal knew that time was of the essence, for how long would it be before the cavalry returned? He could not have thought it would be his own. Perhaps the dead and dying would have disturbed his advancing line more so than it did the Romans. This seems the most reasonable answer.

The Roman army redeployed with the surviving hastati maniples in the middle, flanked by the principes and finally anchored at the flanks by the maniples of the triarii. Perhaps this was done because Scipio saw Hannibal's last line expand and understood that he was being outflanked. It may be that he decided to have his veteran maniples clash with the weakest part of Hannibal's last line, the surviving mercenaries and Carthaginians on the flanks. What mattered most to Scipio was that his badly depleted centre held against Hannibal's 'old guard'. Why he did not place his principes at the centre of his army is interesting. It seems most likely that Scipio intended to have his predominantly fresh veterans crush Hannibal's weaker wings, which consisted of the survivors of the two previous lines, and then entrap Hannibal in the centre. The key was for the hastati, the youngest of the line infantry, to do their job once again and hold out against Hannibal's veterans of the 'Army of Italy'.

We do not know if Hannibal adjusted his lines, but surely he must have seen the new deployment of the legions. We assume Hannibal did not make any tactical changes so that his veterans faced the unused triarii and principes. The presence of survivors from the first and second line on his wings would have made this a very difficult task: moving thousands of men around would certainly have resulted in disruptions to cohesiveness. Hannibal may very well have planned to punch through the Roman centre and then roll up the enemy lines, using his strongest troops. His left flank may have been threatened by the Numidian foot, although there is no written evidence for this. Common sense tells us that a few thousand Roman soldiers could not bear the brunt of the fighting against 20,000, if not more, fighters. So either the Numidians or the principes (or both) were involved, or there were far fewer Carthaginians opposing them than stated. Perhaps it was a combination of the two. Hannibal's tactics seemed to have worked so far. The hastati and velites had suffered greatly from his elephants and his first two lines. Scipio's principes must also have taken some casualties. The remnants of Hannibal's two lines, at least those who did not flee, added numbers to his flanks and extended his last line. As long as the Romano-Numidian cavalry remained away from the field of battle, Hannibal stood every chance of achieving another victory.

Baal Hammon, the chief god of Carthage, sitting on his throne. This statue, now in the National Bardo Museum, Tunis, was discovered in the Thinissut neo-Punic sanctuary (in the Bir Bouregba region). Tanit was the female cult partner of Hammon.

THE CLIMAX OF THE BATTLE

According to Polybius the Roman front line had by now bested 20,000 or more enemy soldiers with a unit only about a quarter of their size. These very men, the survivors of the hastati maniples, now faced the centre of Hannibal's veterans, and Polybius comments that the two sides were 'nearly equal in numbers, spirit, courage, and arms'. As noted previously, Hannibal's last line extended as it grew in number while the Scipian legions were reduced in number and had to reform their line. Polybius describes the climax of the battle:

> The two lines charged each other with the greatest fire and fury ... the battle was for a long time undecided, the men in their obstinate valour falling dead without giving way a step; until at last the divisions of Masinissa and Laelius, returning from the pursuit, arrived providentially in the very nick of time. Upon their charging Hannibal's rear, the greater part of his men were cut down in their ranks; while of those who attempted to fly very few escaped with their life, because the horsemen were close at their heels and the ground was quite level. On the Roman side there fell over 1,500, on the Carthaginian over 20,000, while the prisoners taken were almost as numerous. (Polybius 15.14)

We may assume that most of the casualties occurred during this final clash, for Polybius tells us that this was the hardest fighting. The mercenary and Carthaginian lines gave a good account of themselves. If we are to accept that 20,000 Carthaginians lost their lives and, knowing that the majority of casualties come when one side is routed, we can assume that the first two Carthaginian lines must have suffered thousands of casualties and as such the Roman first rank suffered similarly. Perhaps half of the maniples were combat ineffective. Hypothetically, the front rank might have been reduced by half with mostly wounded not killed. Three thousand formed the centrepiece of Scipio's army then, again reforming into 120-men units; about 25 maniples were left. To their wings then, and evenly split, are the fresh principes of 40 maniples numbering roughly between 4,800 and 6,500 men, though probably fewer due to casualties whilst steadying the hastati against the Carthaginian citizens' charge. To their flanks stood the rested veterans of 2,400 triarii, assuming that these maniples were not larger than 60 men each. This then would give about 10,200–11,900 foot soldiers facing Hannibal's last line. According to these calculations, the two lines would be equal in number, as Polybius writes.

The Battle of Zama, a fresco by the Italian painter Roviale Spagnolo (1511–82). The original can be viewed at the Capitoline Museums, Rome, Italy.

The large number of casualties that Masinissa's Numidians suffered is unlikely to have occurred during the cavalry clash; instead, these casualties must have occurred during the various stages of infantry combat. The lowest number of Numidian cavalry in the clash was around 4,000 versus 2,000 and it is unlikely that this clash would have created a casualty rate of 60 per cent, and we know that light cavalry tends to melt away when defeated. We must remember the 6,000 Numidian foot, and the casualties bear out that they must have had their fair share of the fight. Some of them probably joined their own light cavalry, and others may have fought and dealt with the elephants. But the Numidian foot looks likely to have borne the brunt of the casualties inflicted by Hannibal's three lines. The Numidians started on the right and remained on the far right even after Scipio's realignment, adding thousands of soldiers to the final phase of the battle.

An engraving by Thomassinus after Raphael, dated 1650, showing Scipio's victory over Hannibal at Zama. We can clearly see the massed cavalry charging at the infantry, thus ending any possibility of a Carthaginian victory. (Anne S. K. Brown Military Collection, Brown University Library)

Some considerable time must have passed since the departure of the Carthaginian cavalry wings, and at this point it is worth returning to this opening phase of the battle. The Carthaginian cavalry on both flanks was driven off by a combination of rampaging elephants and by the actions of Masinissa and Laelius, who exploited the situation or who may have been lured away by the loyal Carthaginian cavalry wings. It is possible that Hannibal desired to move his cavalry off and away from the battlefield because a straightforward cavalry fight was most likely unwinnable; the onus of battle could thus rest with the infantry instead. One can easily see how in the confusion of the elephant and cavalry skirmish this deliberate withdrawal is interpreted as flight. The romantic wishes to see the older, brilliant tactician, who had all but lost everything, outwit his younger opponent. And one can argue that Hannibal's intent then was to lure and grind down the two ranks of the Scipian army in the quagmire of the mercenary and citizen lines. Moreover, as the Roman line shrank and more and more maniples joined the fight, Hannibal's last rank was steadily growing and extending; a final push would surround the Romans while Hannibal's fresh and experienced combat veterans crushed the exhausted and tiring Roman centre before the enemy cavalry could return. We know Hannibal kept his third line further back, possibly to avoid being attacked on its flanks by the triarii thus preserving his own tactical ability to launch flanking attacks should the Romans get bogged down in the centre. Polybius's comment about the divisions of Masinissa and Laelius returning from the pursuit 'providentially in the very nick of time' is of particular relevance here.

The final clash of infantry arms 'between equals' leads us to believe that Hannibal's third line of veterans was smaller than the 12,000 mentioned. Of the first two ranks numbering 20,000–24,000, many probably retired to the rear to flock around Hannibal's veterans. Many may also have fled. Some

HANNIBAL'S VETERANS CLASH WITH THE ROMAN HASTATI CENTRE (PP. 80–81)

Hannibal's veterans and survivors from the first and second lines comprising mercenaries and Carthaginian citizens clashed with Scipio's reorganised legions and his Numidian allied infantry. The centre of the line consisted of veteran campaigners (**1**) pitted against the depleted ranks of the hastati (**2**). Spearmen and swordsmen of many nationalities attempted to break the Roman infantry, under the watchful eye of Hannibal and his staff (**3**). This contest of arms was an infantry battle only, as the cavalry had long since left the field and was continuing its skirmishing to Hannibal's rear.

The Roman soldier, according to Polybius, needed a 2.75m space to effectively use his weapon and shield. The hastati maniple spread as it engaged the enemy and, on both sides, the more aggressive soldiers initiated hand-to-hand combat (**4**) as the two lines closed.

scholars have argued that Scipio's army was overlapping Hannibal's and that in fact Hannibal's army was much smaller than the ancients have us believe (Liddell Hart 1992, p. 188).

If we are to estimate the approximate numbers of the Scipian army at this stage, we may presume the following (from the left flank to the right viewed from Hannibal's perspective): *c*.3,000–4,000 Numidians with perhaps a very loose 500–600-man front; the 1,200 triarii presenting a 200-man front that was six–men deep (though three ranks may also have been possible, but dangerous, considering they were facing deeper enemy ranks); the principes, perhaps 2,000–2,500 strong with a minimum 333-man frontage; the surviving 25 hastati maniples of about 3,000 men with a 500-man front; the principes, again with a 333-man front; and lastly, anchored on the far right, the triarii, again numbering around 1,200 with a 200-man width. The velites were most likely spread throughout the rear and possibly also safeguarded the flanks of Scipio's consular army. An estimate of the Romano-Numidian infantry's strength would present *c*.12,400–13,400 men not including velites, and they may have presented a flexible and fluid 2,000–2,100-fighter front. If we are to exclude the Numidian foot, the Roman manipular strength would have presented a *c*.1,600-man front. Assuming a frontage of 2,000–2,100 fighting men and given Polybius' combat diameter of 2.75 metres, then the entire length of the Romano-Numidian line could have stretched to approximately 5.5km. Of course this does not take into account that the triarii fought more akin to a classical hoplite phalanx or that the Numidians may have fought

A modern bust of Scipio in Cartagena, Spain. For his victory over Hannibal and Carthage he was awarded the surname Africanus. (Michelle Ricci)

closer to one another. Again we are left to hypothesise. Nonetheless, the front of the opposing armies increased and extended as the battle progressed.

Whatever the formations and the numbers, we do know that Hannibal's last line did not immediately yield and that the casualties they inflicted on the Romans and Numidians was significant. We can assume that the majority of these were inflicted in the final shield-to-shield, sword-to-sword clash.

As the battle drew to its climactic finale, we should try to imagine the scene before us. Dead bodies littered the ground as the Romano-Numidian single line advanced over them. Most likely the hastati and principes were in open order while the triarii preserved their spear-based, tightly formed phalanxes. The Numidians were also in open order. The velites were spread throughout the rear of the line, perhaps some even still handling captured elephants, moving or despatching wounded soldiers as their comrades advanced past the

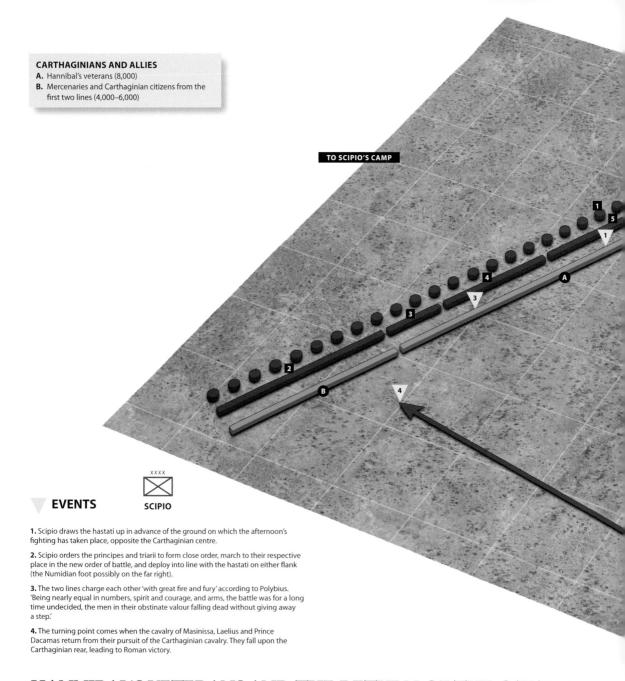

CARTHAGINIANS AND ALLIES
A. Hannibal's veterans (8,000)
B. Mercenaries and Carthaginian citizens from the first two lines (4,000–6,000)

TO SCIPIO'S CAMP

▼ **EVENTS**

⊠
xxxx
SCIPIO

1. Scipio draws the hastati up in advance of the ground on which the afternoon's fighting has taken place, opposite the Carthaginian centre.

2. Scipio orders the principes and triarii to form close order, march to their respective place in the new order of battle, and deploy into line with the hastati on either flank (the Numidian foot possibly on the far right).

3. The two lines charge each other 'with great fire and fury' according to Polybius. 'Being nearly equal in numbers, spirit and courage, and arms, the battle was for a long time undecided, the men in their obstinate valour falling dead without giving away a step.'

4. The turning point comes when the cavalry of Masinissa, Laelius and Prince Dacamas return from their pursuit of the Carthaginian cavalry. They fall upon the Carthaginian rear, leading to Roman victory.

HANNIBAL'S VETERANS AND THE RETURN OF THE CAVALRY: EARLY AFTERNOON

Hannibal's veterans, composing the third and final line, were joined by the survivors of the first and second lines on the flanks. During a short lull in the battle the Romans removed their dead and dying comrades and debris from the field of battle – 'The ground slippery with gore, the corpses lying piled up in bloody heaps, and with the corpses arms flung about in every direction' (Polybius 15.14). The Roman centre was composed of the battered survivors of the hastati, flanked by the principes, who were in turn flanked by the triarii. The Numidian foot most likely remained on the far right flank of Scipio's legions. Here the two lines clashed with the 'greatest fire and fury … equal in spirit, courage and arms'. The fight was for a long time undecided and Polybius says that the arrival of Masinissa and Laelius in the Carthaginian rear was 'in the nick of time', leading to a Roman victory.

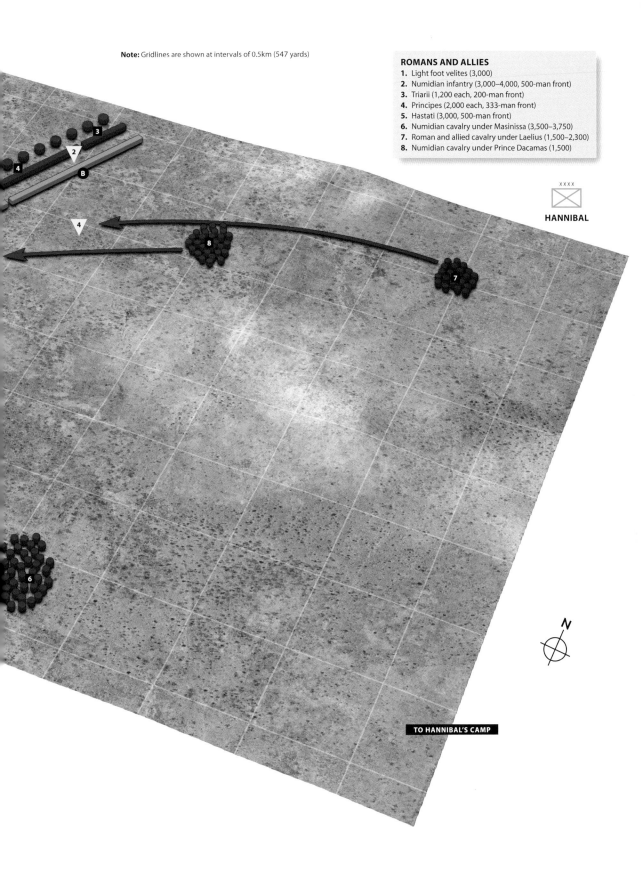

Note: Gridlines are shown at intervals of 0.5km (547 yards)

ROMANS AND ALLIES

1. Light foot velites (3,000)
2. Numidian infantry (3,000–4,000, 500-man front)
3. Triarii (1,200 each, 200-man front)
4. Principes (2,000 each, 333-man front)
5. Hastati (3,000, 500-man front)
6. Numidian cavalry under Masinissa (3,500–3,750)
7. Roman and allied cavalry under Laelius (1,500–2,300)
8. Numidian cavalry under Prince Dacamas (1,500)

HANNIBAL

TO HANNIBAL'S CAMP

dead and dying. The blood and gore must have added a metallic scent to the air. The lines advanced towards one another for the final carnage, amid the cries and sounds of battle.

Perhaps at this time, just prior to the clash, the majority of the men knew that they had to give their utmost. Failure here would bring death or slavery.

At some point both lines charged one another. Pila, javelins and spears were thrown or used in close-quarter battle until swords were drawn and blows exchanged between individual groups.

The fight must have lasted for hours. On the Romano-Numidian side we can well imagine the fury of the Numidians, who along with the triarii and perhaps a few principes were facing mercenaries, Carthaginian citizens and Liby-Phoenicians. The depleted hastati maniples must have suffered the bulk of the Roman casualties as they now faced a fresh, veteran, battle-hardened and unforgiving force of Hannibal's old guard. They now clearly bore the brunt of the fighting in the Scipian army along with the Numidians.

The lines clashed and weapons caused horrible wounds. Most of the Romano-Numidian casualties occurred during this final fight – a tribute to the excellence of Carthaginian arms. Polybius describes 'the men in their obstinate valour falling dead without giving way a step', killing and being killed where they stood and fought – a spectacle of human butchery. It must

Sophoniba, a member of the Carthaginian royalty, was originally married to Syphax to strengthen the bond between the Numidian king and Carthage. Upon Syphax's capture, Masinissa married her on account of her great beauty, much to the displeasure of Scipio, who insisted on her being sent to Rome for his triumph. Masinissa provided her with poison, which she gladly took to avoid the humiliation Scipio had planned. The painting is by Andrea Casali (1705–84) and dates from 1743. It currently resides at Runcorn Town Hall, Cheshire, UK.

have been a shocking sight – sharp and dulled weapons hacking off body parts, slicing through skin, muscle and bone.

One wonders how the battle-weary hastati fared at the height of the final clash. Clearly Hannibal's veterans were superior in experience, arms and steadfastness. Perhaps they sensed they were about to claim victory, with its accompanying spoils with which they might retire in North Africa, telling tall tales of war and conquest to their friends and families. Just one more push, one more Roman death and victory was to be there for the taking. However, rumblings hit the line that Hannibal and others were leaving, fleeing the field of battle. The hastati, however, knew nothing of this; they were in the death throes with the old guard and must have been near breaking point.

Hannibal may very well have been on the brink of victory, for Polybius writes that the Romano-Numidian cavalry arrived in the nick of time. With the arrival of thousands of horsemen in the rear of the Carthaginian army, all became lost. No doubt, soldiers fled where they could, but it seems that the Carthaginian old guard fought to the bitter end, selling their lives dearly – the Romano-Numidian casualties speak of their desperate valour. Some may have survived, but their fate, as well as that of others taken prisoner, was sealed.

One can well imagine the sweat-drenched, bloodied bodies of the survivors being surrounded and killed while others surrendered and were disarmed. Numidian cavalry hunted down those attempting to escape and either butchered them on the spot or captured them to be sold into slavery.

The final casualties are disputed. Polybius and Livy give the Carthaginian losses as 20,000 killed and 20,000 captured. Appian gives 25,000 killed with 8,500 captured. Lazenby believes Appian's numbers to be closer to the truth (1998, p. 225). Roman losses, the ancient authors tell us, were between 1,500 and 2,500 with the Numidians suffering 2,500 killed and 1,500 wounded but far more than the Romans. Goldsworthy dismisses the higher numbers, arguing that 1,500 was equivalent to $c.5$ per cent of the Scipian army and was thus a huge loss (Goldsworthy 2000, p. 307). Of course, the Roman legions had taken massive losses previously, so there is no reason to be dismissive of the higher totals. The total number of wounded is unknown.

Hannibal's camp was sacked by the victorious Romano-Numidians. Soon thereafter the Scipian army marched to Tunis, a short distance from Carthage. At Tunis the victors were able to recover and refit after their arduous campaign.

It was a close-run thing for Scipio. Hannibal was near victory with a decent army, facing one that was perhaps better trained. Were it not for Masinissa's desire for a kingdom, and for the courage and sacrifice of the Numidians, Hannibal may well have emerged victorious and Carthage would have enjoyed a few more years before Rome was ready to send another consular army to challenge the Phoenician city-state.

Knowing the battle was lost, Hannibal escaped to Hadrumetum where his army had previously landed. Here he was able to gather another army composed of survivors from the battle, along with many Bruttian and Iberian horsemen. More levies were recruited here as well within a few short days. The war could have continued, perhaps with the same result as at Zama, but it was clear to all, including Hannibal Barca, that Carthage must now sue for peace.

AFTERMATH

The battle of Zama was the last great battle of the Second Punic War. The presence of Masinissa nullified Hannibal's strength in cavalry, while Hannibal's tactical awareness nullified the Roman ability to execute tactical changes during the battle in an attempt to envelop Hannibal's army, as Scipio had done against other Carthaginian commanders. The ancient accounts tell us that Hannibal's army was shattered after a long period of holding their ground, despite being on the brink of victory.

How are we to judge the performances of the two great commanders? The ancient sources only present fragments of the entire tale. They are pro-Roman and what remains of their writing on Zama is certainly pro-Scipian. However, there is no doubt that the legend of Hannibal, which endures even to this day, heavily influenced their writing and some of their comments about the Carthaginian are highly positive. Nonetheless, we have no Carthaginian records of the war and the battle to help identify balance and bias in the pro-Roman accounts.

According to the ancient sources, Scipio outwitted and outfought Hannibal. The use of flank attacks, ruses, surprise attacks and the manoeuvring of maniples during the battle certainly proved Scipio to be an excellent general. Also, he was not shy to use all means possible, fair or foul, in his attempt to gain the upper hand, as witnessed in the night-time

An atmospheric view of the Tunisian landscape, looking towards the Jugurtha Tableland, near the town of Kalaat es Senam in the Kef Governate. The fortress (*qalat*) atop the Jugurtha Tableland mesa sits at an altitude of 1,255m. Legend has it that Masinissa built the first fortress on this site around 200 BC. (Slim Alileche)

attack on the Carthaginian camps and while negotiations were underway. For Scipio this was a personal war, much as it was for Hannibal. Both had lost close family members. What is more, for Scipio the final battle of the Second Punic War meant a reunion with his disgraced soldiers of Cannae, offering them redemption and a place in history alongside him.

Hannibal on the other hand must surely have envisioned the battle as the culmination of years of fighting for himself and his veterans. Even if victorious, most, if not all, of the latter might well have seen the time as right to retire in North Africa alongside their glorious commander. However, any respite would only have been temporary. Had Hannibal won at Zama – and he came close – more consular armies would have arrived on the North African shores, such was Rome's determination to eliminate its foe.

It can be argued that the battle was not won by Scipio but by the Africans under Masinissa. Their losses of over 4,000 dead and wounded – well in excess of the 1,500–2,500 Roman dead – speak of the impact the Numidians had on the battle, and the utmost savagery, if not hatred, they exhibited in combat towards the Carthaginians. Masinissa, arguably, was the true victor and would build a unified Numidian kingdom. He lived to be an old man, seeing the Third Punic War begin but not end. Carthage had to be destroyed for his kingdom to be dominant.

It is hard to reconcile the ancient sources regarding the immediate events following the battle. Polybius's assertion regarding the complete annihilation of the Carthaginian army conflicts with the later accounts given by Appian and Nepos. Appian says that Hannibal took refuge in a town called Thon, where he found many Bruttians and Iberian horsemen who had fled after the defeat. Nepos writes that at Hadrumetum Hannibal rallied the survivors of the retreat and by means of new levies mustered a large number of soldiers within a few days. Any Roman deserters captured at Zama would have been beheaded, or if citizens of Rome crucified. The rest of Hannibal's captured army was probably sold into slavery.

Carthage sent envoys to Scipio in Tunis to seek an armistice and Polybius tells us that Scipio showed no regard for their lamentations:

For they ought not to consider it a hardship if they found themselves charged to submit to any punishment, to follow a particular line of conduct, or to give up this or that; they ought rather to regard it as an unexpected favour that any kindness was conceded to them at all; since Fortune, after depriving them of all right to pity and consideration, owing to their own unrighteous conduct, had put them in the power of their enemies. (Polybius 15.17)

The interesting note here is that the wars fought with Carthage were started by Rome. Polybius again is our source for the terms put upon Carthage. He does note that the terms offered some favourable points to the vanquished:

The Carthaginians [were] to retain the towns in Libya, of which they were possessed before they commenced the last war against Rome, and the territory which they also heretofore held, with its cattle, slaves, and other stock: and from that day should not be subject to acts of hostility, should enjoy their own laws and customs, and not have a Roman garrison in their city. These were the concessions favourable to them. (Polybius 15.18)

The unfavourable clauses were as follows:

The Carthaginians [were] to pay an indemnity to the Romans for all wrongs committed during the truce; to restore all captives and runaway slaves without limit of time; to hand over all their ships of war except ten triremes, and all elephants; to go to war with no people outside Libya at all, and with none in Libya without consent from Rome; to restore to Masinissa all houses, territory, and cities belonging to him or his ancestors within the frontiers assigned to that king; to supply the Roman army with provisions for three months, and with pay, until such time as an answer shall be returned from Rome on the subject of the treaty; to pay 10,000 talents of silver in 50 years, 200 Euboic talents every year; to give 100 hostages of their good faith—such hostages to be selected from the young men of the country by the Roman general, and to be not younger than 14 or older than 30 years. (Polybius 15.18)

A view of the landscape looking north over the outskirts of the town of Tajerouine, which lies c.15km to the south of the most likely location of the battle of Zama. (Ahmed Ettoro)

Although the terms were harsh, Scipio was ill equipped for a long siege of Carthage. In effect his hands were tied by his inability to conclude the war emphatically. Of course, his intention may not have been to seek the total destruction of his life-long enemy, but military reality on the ground and the costs in manpower and finances alone would have made a siege nearly impossible – very much like Hannibal's inability to besiege Rome after his victory at Cannae 14 years earlier. Moreover, Carthage still had a large army under Hannibal's command that could threaten the besieging army. In any event, whichever motivations may have underlined Scipio's decision we do know from the ancient sources that the Carthaginians were given three months to send envoys to Rome to end the war. But Carthage was not yet prepared to accept the terms. Perhaps they remembered their famous Spartan mercenary captain Xanthippus, who was hired after Rome insisted on harsh terms many decades previously and who defeated a consular army in 255 BC.

When the terms where brought to the senate of Carthage, a politican named Gisgo objected vociferously. Hannibal was present during the discussions and forcefully removed Gisgo from the speaker's platform. Livy's account of Hannibal's conduct continues:

> This was an unusual sight in a free community, and the people were loud in their disapproval. The soldier, taken aback by the free expression of opinion on the part of his fellow citizens, said, 'I left you when I was 9 years old, and now after 36 years' absence I have returned. The art of war which I have been taught from my boyhood, first as a private soldier and then in high command, I think I am fairly well acquainted with. The rules and laws and customs of civic life and of the forum I must learn from you.' After this apology for his inexperience, he discussed the terms of peace and showed that they were not unreasonable and that their acceptance was a necessity. (Livy 30.37)

Surely Hannibal must have understood that the terms Rome forced upon Carthage, only allowing them defensive capabilities and forbidding the waging of war on its neighbours, meant that Carthaginian hegemony had permanently ended. Any future war against Masinissa's offensive operations to expand his kingdom would immediately see the return of Roman legions to North African shores and possibly a permanent end for Carthage.

Hannibal, a life-long soldier, could have continued the war but chose peace, no matter how painful it was for Carthage. He may have been a son of Carthage, but later events would prove that Carthage's love for her son had its limits. Moreover, the peace granted by Rome to Carthage was as short-lived as the time it took Rome to execute further conquests in the Eastern Mediterranean.

After peace had been negotiated, and was finally ratified by Rome in 201 BC, Hannibal became a civil magistrate in Carthage. However, internecine squabbles led to his denouncement by his Carthaginian enemies. Taking flight, Hannibal sought refuge in various kingdoms embroiled in war against Rome or its allies. He eventually settled with Prusias I of Bithynia, who at that time was engaged in war with Rome's ally, King Eumenes II of Pergamum. He served Prusias in his war, but soon grew wary of Bithynian treachery. One day he sent out a faithful servant to check all the exits from his fortress at Libyssa. The

This engraving by Dambrun from a drawing by Silvestre David Mirys (1742–1810) shows Hannibal about to drink poison. His right foot rests on a captured Roman standard, which serves as a reminder that Hannibal was Rome's greatest enemy.

Rome's rise and the decline of Carthage, 202–146 BC.

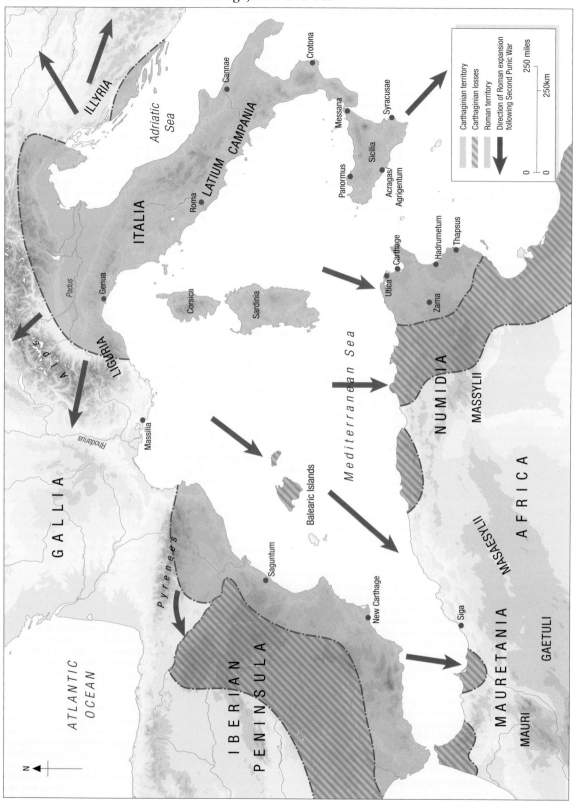

Legend:
- Carthaginian territory
- Carthaginian losses
- Roman territory
- Direction of Roman expansion following Second Punic War

250 miles
250km

ILLYRIA

Adriatic Sea

Crotona
Cannae
ITALIA
LATIUM
CAMPANIA
Roma
Messana
Syracusae
Sicilia
Panormus
Acragas/Agrigentum

Corsica
Sardinia

Padus
Genua
LIGURIA

A l p e s

Rhodanus
Massilia

GALLIA

Pyrenees

Saguntum

Balearic Islands

New Carthage

Mediterranean Sea

Utica
Carthage
Hadrumetum
Thapsus
Zama
NUMIDIA
MASSYLII

AFRICA
MASAESYLII
Siga
MAURETANIA
MAURI
GAETULI

IBERIAN PENINSULA

ATLANTIC OCEAN

N

servant reported back that guards stood at every exit. Knowing that he had been betrayed and was unable to escape, Hannibal poisoned himself in a final act of defiance. The year is uncertain but was probably 183 BC.

Scipio initially fared better than Hannibal. The victorious general, the conqueror of the Carthaginians, returned to Sicily with his army. He then made his way up through southern Italy and on to Rome. Livy paints a vivid picture of the returning hero, who travelled through:

> multitudes who poured out from the cities to do him honour, and crowds of peasants who blocked the roads in the country districts. The triumphal procession in which he rode into the city was the most brilliant that had ever been seen. The weight of silver which he brought into the treasury amounted to 123,000 pounds. Out of the booty he distributed 40 ases to each soldier. Syphax had died shortly before at Tibur … [but this] in no way dimmed the glory of the triumphing general … As to the sobriquet of Africanus, whether it was conferred upon him by the devotion of his soldiers or by the popular breath, or … it originated in the flattery of his friends, I cannot say for certain. At all events, he was the first commander-in-chief who was ennobled by the name of the people he had conquered. (Livy 30.45)

In later years in Rome, Scipio's political opponents, led by the elder Cato, launched a series of attacks on the Scipios and their supporters, even though they successfully defeated the Seleucids in 190 BC. Scipio continued to oppose Rome's desire to hunt down Hannibal. He withdrew from Rome to Liternum in Campania, where he led a simple life in a country villa farming the land. He passed away in 184 or 183 BC, a virtual exile.

One of the unintended consequences of the Second Punic War was that Rome became an oligarchy and the sovereignty of the Roman people became subordinated to the will of the senate. Between 233 BC and 133 BC, out of 200 consulships 159 were held by 26 noble families, and half were held by 10 families (Cook et al. 1981, pp. 110–11).

Masinissa had firmly established himself as king of the Numidian tribes of the Massylii and the Masaesylii and set about consolidating and strengthening his kingdom, much to the displeasure of a weakened Carthage. He made sure that Rome extended protection to his new kingdom, and a clause in the peace treaty of 201 BC between Rome and Carthage forbade the latter from going to war with the Numidians, unless expressly approved by Rome first. Masinissa gradually gained more territory from Carthage and tensions would continue to exist until the events of the Third Punic War (149–146 BC). Masinissa died in 148 BC aged 90, two years before Carthage was ploughed into the ground by the Romans.

The tomb of Masinissa at El-Khroub, in Constantine Province, Algeria. (Yellès Arif)

FURTHER READING

Abbott, J., *Hannibal: Warrior and Statesman*, D.M. Maclellan Book Company, New York, 1900

Adcock, F. E., *The Greek and Macedonian Art of War*, University of California Press, Berkeley, 1957

Appian (trans. White, H.), *The Punic Wars* [website] <http://www.livius.org/ap-ark/appian/appian_punic_19.html#%A795>, accessed 1 July 2015

Cook, S. A., Adcock, F. E. and Charlesworth, M. P. (eds.), *The Cambride Ancient History*, Vol. VIII: *Rome and the Mediterranean 218–133 BC*, Cambridege University Press, Cambridge, 1981

Delbrück, H., *Warfare in Antiquity*, Vol. 1, University of Nebraska Press, Lincoln, 1990

Fields, N., *The Roman Army in the Punic Wars 264–146 BC*, Osprey Publishing, Oxford, 2007

——, *Roman Conquests: North Africa*, Pen & Sword, Barnsley, 2010

Friha, N., *The Legendary Story of the Founding of Carthage-Byrsa* [website] <http://unstats.un.org/unsd/geoinfo/UNGEGN/docs/26th-gegn-docs/Essay%20poem/1_FRIHA.pdf>, accessed 26 June 2015

Goldsworthy, A., *The Fall of Carthage*, Cassell, London, 2000

Hoyos, D., *Hannibal: Rome's Greatest Enemy*, Bristol Phoenix Press, Exeter, 2008

—— (ed.), *A Companion to the Punic Wars*, Wiley-Blackwell, Oxford, 2011

——, *Mastering the West: Rome and Carthage at War*, Oxford University Press, New York, 2015

Hunt, P., *Hannibal's Ethnicity and Physical Appearance* [website] <http://www.britannica.com/topic/Hannibals-ethnicity-and-physical-appearance-2020107>, accessed 2015

Ilevbare, J. A., *Carthage, Rome and the Berbers*, Ibadan University Press, Ibadan, Nigeria, 1981

Kromayer, J. and Veith, G., *Antike Schlachtfelder: Bausteine zu einer antiken Kriegsgeschichte*, Weidmann, Berlin, 1903

Lago Marin, J. I., *La Batalla de Zama 202 A.C.*, Almena Ediciones, 2013

Lazenby, J. F., *Hannibal's War: A Military History of the Second Punic War*, University of Oklahoma Press, 1998

Lendon, J. E., *Ghosts and Soldiers*, Yale University Press, New Haven, 2001

Liddell Hart, B. H., *Scipio Africanus: Greater Than Napoleon*, Greenhill Books, London, 1992

Livy, *The History of Rome*, available at *Titus Livius: The History of Rome* [website] <http://mcadams.posc.mu.edu/txt/ah/Livy>, accessed 2015

MacDonald, E., *Hannibal: A Hellenistic Life*, Yale University Press, New Haven, 2015

Nossov, K., *War Elephants*, Osprey Publishing Ltd., Oxford, 2008

Picard, G. C. and Picard, C., (trans. Collon, D.) *Carthage: A Survey of Punic History and Culture from its Birth to the Final Tragedy*, Sedgwick & Jackson, London, 1987

Polybius (trans. Paton, W. R.), *The Histories*, Loeb Classical Library, Harvard University Press, 1922–27; available at *The Histories of Polybius* [website] <http://penelope.uchicago.edu/Thayer/E/Roman/Texts/Polybius/home.html>, accessed 2015

Riddehough, G. B., 'The Mercenaries of Ancient Carthage', MA Thesis, University of British Columbia, 1939

Soren, D. and Slim, H., *Carthage: From the Legends of The Aeneid to the Glorious Age of Gold: An Engrossing History of the Vanished Empire that Rivaled Athens and Rome*, Touchstone Books, New York, 1990

Van Wees, H., *Greek Warfare: Myths and Realities*, Gerald Duckworth & Co. Ltd., London, 2004

Walbank, F. W., *A Historical Commentary on Polybius*, Vol. II, Oxford University Press, Oxford, 1967

Warry, J., *Warfare in the Classical World*, St. Martin's Press, New York, 1980

INDEX